Manifestation

Unlock the Power of Manifesting Your Dreams through Secret Formulas, Quantum Jumping, Visualizations, 369, Affirmations, and More

© Copyright 2025 - All rights reserved.

The content contained within this book may not be reproduced, duplicated, or transmitted without direct written permission from the author or the publisher.

Under no circumstances will any blame or legal responsibility be held against the publisher or author for any damages, reparation, or monetary loss due to the information contained within this book, either directly or indirectly.

Legal Notice:

This book is copyright-protected. It is only for personal use. You cannot amend, distribute, sell, use, quote, or paraphrase any part of the content within this book without the consent of the author or publisher.

Disclaimer Notice:

Please note the information contained within this document is for educational and entertainment purposes only. All effort has been executed to present accurate, up-to-date, reliable, and complete information. No warranties of any kind are declared or implied. Readers acknowledge that the author is not engaging in the rendering of legal, financial, medical, or professional advice. The content within this book has been derived from various sources. Please consult a licensed professional before attempting any techniques outlined in this book.

By reading this document, the reader agrees that under no circumstances is the author responsible for any losses, direct or indirect, that are incurred as a result of the use of the information contained within this document, including, but not limited to, errors, omissions, or inaccuracies.

Your Free Gift
(only available for a limited time)

Thanks for getting this book! If you want to learn more about various spirituality topics, then join Mari Silva's community and get a free guided meditation MP3 for awakening your third eye. This guided meditation mp3 is designed to open and strengthen ones third eye so you can experience a higher state of consciousness. Simply visit the link below the image to get started.

https://spiritualityspot.com/meditation
Or, Scan the QR code!

Table of Contents

INTRODUCTION 1
CHAPTER 1: DECODING MANIFESTATION BASICS 3
CHAPTER 2: SHAPING YOUR MANIFESTATION MINDSET 16
CHAPTER 3: CREATING YOUR MANIFESTATION TOOLKIT 30
CHAPTER 4: VISUALIZING THE LIFE YOU WANT 47
CHAPTER 5: AFFIRMATIONS FOR SCRIPTING A NEW REALITY 58
CHAPTER 6: THE 369 METHOD AND OTHER SECRET MANIFESTATION FORMULAS 71
CHAPTER 7: QUANTUM JUMPING AND REALITY SHIFTING 83
CHAPTER 8: DAILY MANIFESTATION RITUALS AND ROUTINES 95
CONCLUSION 107
HERE'S ANOTHER BOOK BY MARI SILVA THAT YOU MIGHT LIKE 110
YOUR FREE GIFT (ONLY AVAILABLE FOR A LIMITED TIME) 111
REFERENCES 112
IMAGE SOURCES 124

Introduction

Being wealthy, lasting love, and the rekindling of relationships are among the most common themes of manifestation, but most people have doubts about how to achieve them. Manifestation is very tricky to work with. In essence, it is the practice of transmitting your thoughts and ideas into reality. It involves setting more pronounced intentions and accompanying them with clear visualizations of your goal. Most people think that manifestation is magic and that they'll wake up to find that their visualizations have come to life.

However, if you work a minimum wage job, you won't become a millionaire overnight, even if you have manifested and clearly visualized this desire. Manifestation will keep you focused on your goals, open new doors, reduce the roadblocks you encounter, and direct you toward the right opportunities and people. It's up to you to stay determined, build discipline, take actionable steps, and make the most out of the tools, people, and opportunities that come your way.

As you manifest and visualize your desires, work on building skills like self-confidence, self-control, and determination. When you add effort to your intention, you will likely achieve better results. Manifestation also requires you to take control of your thoughts and feelings and do your best to keep a positive mindset. It helps to break down your goals, determine your actions to get there, and trust that opportunities will start popping up out of nowhere.

Serving as a comprehensive guide to effective manifestation techniques, this is the only book about manifestation you'll ever have to read. In this book, you will find many practical activities and exercises backed by indispensable knowledge and guidance. By the end of this book, you'll have mastered the art of spiritual and psychic communication.

This book will guide you through the core principles of manifestation as it delves into the mechanics of how your thoughts and intentions can be transmitted into reality. You'll learn how to build a strong, positive mindset for manifestation. Then, you will understand how effective visualization can activate your subconscious mind and align your energy with your intentions, and you will learn about vivid visualization techniques.

In this book, you'll also learn about the power of affirmations and understand how you can come up with your own positive statements that you can relate to. You'll learn about the 369 Method, among the most popular and effective manifestation techniques, and other secret manifestation formulas. This book will also introduce you to the concept of quantum jumping and reality shifting, well-versing you on how you can jump into alternate realities or futures to align with your desires. Finally, you'll discover how to incorporate manifestation practices into your daily routine.

Chapter 1: Decoding Manifestation Basics

Close your eyes and envision that you have the power to achieve your goals. Imagine that anything you visualize can become a reality. This isn't magic. It's manifestation. While working hard is crucial to accomplish your dreams, you must also align your thoughts, feelings, beliefs, and actions with your goals. You may struggle if you don't believe in yourself or allow your negative thoughts to make you focus on challenges instead of opportunities.

Manifestation basics are the foundation of your journey to enlightenment.[1]

Manifestation isn't just wishing for something and waiting for it to come true. It is a process that requires taking specific steps that bring you closer to your goal and understanding the impact of your thoughts and intentions on your reality. Manifestation is a great skill that can take you far in life.

This chapter explains concepts such as manifestation, the law of attraction, universal energy, the quantum universe, and the multiverse concept. It also explores the roles of vibration and frequency. You will also discover manifestation formulas and frameworks, the science behind them, the power of belief, and emotional alignment.

Defining Manifestation

The word manifestation means transforming an idea into reality. Manifestation is defined as materializing your desires by aligning your thoughts, feelings, beliefs, and actions with your goals. It is a self-development technique that involves setting intention, repeating positive affirmations, and practicing visualizations. Social psychologist Dr Kinga Mnich describes it as "A holistic approach that brings your desires to life by living your dreams." Therapist Elizabeth Winkler describes it as a creation process that involves self-reflection and discovering the life of your dreams and what you need to do to manifest it.

Manifestation connects the body, mind, and spirit and aligns your energy with the universe. It focuses on releasing negative emotions and thoughts, limiting beliefs, and replacing them with positivity. It requires recognizing one's goals, envisioning success, focusing on the positive, and practicing gratitude to transform your intentions into tangible reality. It is based on the belief that focusing on your desires motivates you to take action and achieve your goals.

Manifestation is more effective when you act like you have already achieved your goals. For instance, if you want to get promoted at work, you should prepare yourself by dressing more professionally, adopting the mindset and habits associated with the new role, and socializing with people holding similar positions. This will show you how it feels to have your goal manifested, motivating you to work hard to achieve it.

Some people argue that manifestation isn't practical. They think it only involves setting intentions and visualization. However, it is a complex process that requires choosing reasonable goals and realistic strategies to focus one's attention and energy on manifesting one's desires.

People who use manifestation understand the significance of the mind in this process. It can transform negative thoughts by influencing the subconscious to think positively. Hence, you start believing in your abilities and chances of success.

Manifestation can be summed up in four words, "ask, believe, and receive." Simply ask the universe for what you want, believe that you have already received it, and you will receive it.

Law of Attraction and Universal Energy

The law of attraction is one of the 12 universal laws, and it suggests that positive energy attracts positive outcomes while negative energy attracts negative outcomes. You can attract anything you want by aligning your energy with the universe. Alignment is matching your energy or vibrational frequency with what you want. It's feeling happy and confident because you are certain that everything you want is coming to you. You aren't worried about how your dreams will manifest. You surrender to the universe and trust its wisdom.

The Law of Attraction's Main Principles

- **Focusing on the Present:** The law of attraction suggests that everyone has the power to improve or alter their present. Most people work hard to have a better future. They believe they can't do anything to change their current circumstances and focus their attention on the future. However, the law indicates that while the present can be flawed, you shouldn't give in or live unhappily. The past is behind you, and the future isn't guaranteed. The present is all you have. So you should use all your effort and energy to make this moment the best it can be.

- **Making Space for Positive Energy:** Releasing negative energy and thoughts makes space for positivity. The law of attraction suggests that the mind is always full, and another must always take its place when you remove something. You should always let go of what doesn't serve you and replace it with what benefits you.

- **Similar Things Attract Each Other:** You attract people, thoughts, and energies similar to you. Negative thoughts can bring negativity to every aspect of your life, while positive thinking can attract positive experiences that can transform your life.

The Law of Attraction Sub-Laws

The law of attraction consists of seven sub-laws.

1. **Manifestation:** This law suggests that you can improve your present by focusing your energy on changing yourself and your life. Obsessing over past mistakes and worrying about the future will not change your life or help you move forward. Working on improving the present is the only way to make peace with the past and prepare for the future.
2. **Harmony:** The harmony and balance in your environment impact your energy. You should tap into this energy to create a positive mindset while working on your goals. You should also surround yourself with like-minded people who inspire, support, and encourage you to accomplish your goals.
3. **Magnetism:** People attract what they think. If you focus on the positive, your perspective will change. You will start seeing an opportunity in every challenge, which will improve your mood and well-being.
4. **Universal Influence:** This is the most important law of attraction principle. It is similar to Newton's third law, " For every action (force) in nature, there is an equal and opposite reaction." What you send out to the world comes back to you. This doesn't only apply to thoughts and emotions but also to behavior. For instance, if you disrespect a coworker, they will treat you the same. If you work hard, you will reap the benefit of your effort. If you are a good person, you will be able to help others and make a difference in the world. As a result, you will influence the universe, and the world will be a better place.
5. **Unwavering Desires:** This law suggests that people should focus on the goals that align with their plans, such as strengthening their relationships, advancing their careers, or exercising to improve their health. You should be aware of your desires and understand that your goals can change at any stage of your life. However, if you know who you are and trust your abilities, you can achieve all your goals.

6. **Delicate Balance:** While some days are good, others can be bad. You may face obstacles, experience failure, or heartbreak. You need to accept that setbacks are a part of life. Celebrate your wins, embrace your losses, and learn from your mistakes.
7. **Right Action:** You may experience situations that can make life challenging, such as an unsatisfying career or a toxic relationship. You may believe there is no way out, and you will be stuck in these situations for the rest of your life. However, this law suggests that you have the power to let go of all the things that hold you back and replace them with your purpose and the skills you need to achieve your goals.

The Role of Frequency and Vibration

The law of attraction suggests that everything and everyone is made of energy operating at different frequencies. To manifest your goals, change the frequency of negative energy with positive energy and thoughts. Use gratitude to recognize all the blessings the universe has bestowed on you. Focus on achieving your goals instead of worrying about failure.

Humans, all other living creatures, and objects are made of cells. Their frequency reflects the speed of these cells' vibrational patterns. Fast or high vibrations mean high energy and frequency, while slow or low vibration means low energy and frequency.

Each person vibrates at a subtle and different frequency. If you are sad or sick, you will vibrate at a lower frequency, while if you are healthy and happy, you will vibrate at a higher frequency.

According to renowned researcher Dr. David R. Hawkins, emotions generate an energy field. He recognized that negative emotions such as hatred, fear, and anger have low frequencies. In contrast, positive emotions such as gratitude, joy, and love have high frequencies.

Similarly, thoughts vibrate at different frequencies. The universe can identify the unique vibrations your thoughts release. For instance, you will never advance in your career if you constantly think you aren't good enough to get promoted. These negative thoughts are released to the universe in the form of frequencies and manifest and become a reality. Although this may seem disconcerting, you can use this information to your advantage.

You should pay attention to the frequencies and vibrations you emit because you will attract situations, experiences, and people that vibrate at a similar frequency. If you train your brain to think positively, you will raise your thought frequencies and manifest what you desire.

You are what you think, and emotions are the by-product of your thoughts. You can experience positive or negative feelings depending on the frequency of these emotions.

Intentions also carry unique frequencies and are extremely powerful – which is exactly why one should set an intention before manifestation to send positive vibrations to the universe and attract what one desires.

Manifestation Formulas and Frameworks

You probably wonder how manifestation works. Do you close your eyes and make a wish? Do you write it down? Manifestation is a process that involves structured formulas and approaches that can help you make your dreams a reality. Manifestation formulas are practical methods that allow you to focus your intentions and energy toward specific goals.

The 369 Manifestation Method

Renowned engineer and inventor Nikola Tesla believed that the numbers three, six, and nine are powerful and hold the keys to understanding the universe. Manifesting with these numbers aligns your goals with the universe, allowing you to tap into its energy and bring your dreams to life.

The 369 manifestation method is a simple technique that involves repeating affirmations that align with your desires three times in the morning, six times in the afternoon, and nine times before bed.

Nikola Tesla believed that the numbers three, six, and nine are powerful.'

The key to this method is consistency. You can't practice the 369 method once a week or whenever you remember it. It should be a part of your daily routine, and you should practice it until your desires are manifested. Consistency is necessary to keep your mind and energy focused on achieving your goals.

Scripting

Scripting is another manifestation approach that allows you to focus your intentions and energy on specific goals. It is a creative process that involves writing down your goals as if you are already living them. You should picture your life if your desires were manifested and describe every detail, thought, and emotion. Make it as vivid as possible. This technique is based on the law of attraction, which states that you can attract positive experiences by focusing on the positive.

You can achieve any manifestation formula with these five techniques.

A Strong Desire

Manifestation begins by recognizing your goals. What are your deepest desires? What consumes your thoughts? What aspects of your life do you want to improve or change? Self-reflect to find what goals you want to achieve. It should be something you need and not a whim. Differentiate between your wants and needs to find your true purpose. Find something significant that transforms your life or makes you feel complete, like a soulmate or a fulfilling career.

Try meditation or journaling if you struggle to find your deepest desire. These techniques clear your mind and help you visualize the life you want. Once you find your goal, focus your energy, thoughts, and emotions on it. This amplifies your manifestation and sends a loud and powerful signal to the universe. The law of attraction suggests that like attracts like. Focusing completely on your desire will attract the experiences, opportunities, and people that bring you closer to your goal.

Positivity

Fuel your desire with positive emotions and thoughts. Sometimes, people feel pessimistic when they think about their goals. For instance, a person who dreams about traveling the world may view this goal with a defeated spirit. Instead of picturing themselves traveling and having fun, they tell themselves, "I will never be able to save money and travel anywhere. I should give up and stop thinking about it." This mindset prevents you from manifesting and making an effort to achieve your goal.

You need to visualize your dream coming true and all the positive emotions you will experience when it does. For instance, if your goal is to find your soulmate, imagine how it feels to be in love and how happy you feel that you have finally found them. Positive emotions are powerful and release a high frequency that resonates with your goals and interacts with the world around you.

Belief

Conviction is key in manifestation. Believe that your desire will be manifested and release any self-doubt. Manifestation goes beyond wishful thinking. Knowing that the universe will turn it into reality once you manifest your desire. Nothing and no one can shake your trust in the process. Remember that whatever you send to the universe will come back to you. A manifestation filled with uncertainties will have low frequency and be ineffective. It is as if you're speaking to someone in a voice so low that they can't hear you.

Believing in what you say and knowing it will be manifested sends a powerful signal to the universe that cannot be ignored.

No Deadline

Manifestation formulas don't have a deadline. If your dreams don't manifest in a few months, this doesn't mean they will never become real. The universe is wise, infinite, and knowledgeable. It doesn't have the same limitations people do, nor does it work within a certain time frame. It has its own process and pace, so be patient. Maybe it wants you to learn a lesson first or experience something to prepare you before you receive your desire.

Many expect their desires to manifest right away. When they don't, they stop manifesting or doubting the universe or their abilities. This can disrupt the manifestation process. Believe that your desires will manifest without worrying about when. Everything is in motion the moment you set your intentions. The universe is preparing opportunities, events, and situations to bring you closer to your goal.

You don't have to understand how the universe works or why it makes you wait. Just trust in the process. Everything happens at the right time and not a moment sooner.

Keep Repeating Affirmations

Affirmations are the foundation of manifestation. The stronger they are, the more powerful your manifestation will be. Don't just say them once and expect your desire to be realized. Each repetition strengthens the vibrations you send to the universe and amplifies your manifestation. Repeat your affirmations every day, even if it takes months or years for your dreams to become a reality.

The Science Behind Manifesting with Thoughts

Most people consider manifestation a spiritual technique. However, others view it from a psychological or scientific approach. They believe that intention and mindset can impact a person's behavior and actions. Neuroscientist Dr. James R. Doty says that manifestation goes beyond sending positive vibrations to the universe. It is a powerful technique that can rewire your brain and train your subconscious to recognize your goals and take the necessary steps to achieve them. Say you hate your current job. Repeating positive affirmations such as, "My career fulfills me and allows me to be creative and express myself," will convince you that you will find a better job that aligns with your passion. This technique strengthens your brain pathways and motivates you to chase your goals. It also teaches your brain to prioritize your dreams so that it becomes focused on making them a reality. Dr. Doty adds that intention and visualization activate your cognitive brain networks and push you to work hard to achieve your goals.

Dr. Doty also explains that the brain creates neural connections based on experiences, emotions, and thoughts. The brain rewires itself through repeated thought patterns, focusing, and expectations.

Psychologist Dr. Carol Dweck echoes Dr. Doty's theories. You are more likely to achieve something if you believe you can do it because you will work harder and won't give up, no matter how many challenges you face.

For instance, if you believe you will get a job, you will research the company, dress nicely for the interview, and confidently answer each question. On the other hand, if you don't believe you will get it, you won't prepare for the interview and give short answers that show your lack of interest in the job.

Psychologist Barbara Fredrickson explains that positive emotions make people more creative. Psychology professor Sonja Lyubomirsky says that happiness leads to success. A positive attitude encourages people to recognize opportunities and see challenges as stepping stones.

According to a 2006 study conducted by Duke University, Fuqua School of Business, Durham, and the National Bureau of Economic Research, Cambridge, optimistic people work hard to achieve their goals. They are usually more financially stable because they save money.

The Placebo Effect

The placebo effect is a phenomenon in which a treatment, such as medication or practicing techniques like manifestation, can make one feel better or provide the desired outcome even though it has no medical or therapeutic effect. These outcomes emphasize the significance of thoughts and beliefs and their impact on one's perception and well-being.

Manifestation is similar to the placebo effect as both show that your beliefs can influence outcomes. Believing that manifestation can help you achieve your goals can affect your mindset, like the placebo effect. While the placebo effect is popular and effective, it has its limitations and can't be applied to every situation. Similarly, manifestation has its boundaries. It makes you resilient, optimistic, motivated, and confident and rewires your brain, but you won't get results without taking action.

You must understand the impact and limitations of manifestation and how it is compared to the placebo effect. While both showcase the impact of beliefs and a positive mindset, you can't depend on them alone. You need to have a plan and work hard on your dreams while believing that the universe will provide the opportunities and people needed to help you achieve them.

Neuroplasticity

Neuroplasticity is the brain's ability to rewire neural connections. Simply, it can make your brain more flexible. Your brain can change and adapt to create different reactions and responses that can benefit you. For instance, you can teach your brain to adjust plans and try again when you fail instead of giving up and feeling defeated. Repeated thought patterns and expectations can influence the brain to shape reality. Intentions, positive thinking, and repeating affirmations can create new circuits in the brain that release thoughts and emotions that no longer serve you and replace them with beneficial ones.

Focusing on the positive can alter your brain and strengthen the parts that can help you learn, act, believe in yourself, and achieve your goals. While your brain adapts to new changes, it will adjust your thought patterns and behavior, bringing positive outcomes.

The Impact of Focused Intention

Focused intention goes beyond repeating positive statements and sending them out to the universe. It is a powerful tool that can pave the way to success. It eliminates negative thoughts, self-doubt, your inner critic, and other people's opinions. It keeps you determined and optimistic, believing nothing can stand between you and your goals. Focused intention is different from regular intentions. You don't just say once what you hope to achieve. You repeat it every day to send strong signals to the universe, attracting people and situations that align with your goal. The more you repeat your intention, the more your brain will realize its significance and shift its attention to that goal to create the desired outcome.

Quantum Universe and the Multiverse Concept

If you are a comic book fan, the multiverse concept may not be new to you. Although it may seem far-fetched, many scientists and physicists claim it is possible. In quantum mechanics, particles can exist in different states simultaneously. According to the multiverse theory, when one state is observed, another quantum outcome becomes a reality in a different world. Thus, the universe branches out different alternatives or realities at each moment; these universes are separate and will never interact with one another. The result? *Different versions of your goals may already exist.*

Quantum Entanglement

Quantum entanglement is the theory that two or more particles can be entangled even if they don't exist in the same place. This led many physicists to believe in the existence of the multiverse. According to physicist Hugh Everet, the universe splits into multiple branches representing various outcomes during quantum measurement. A parallel universe is created in each branch.

Similar to particles being entangled, focusing your emotions, thoughts, and energy on your desire creates an entanglement with it.

The Observer Effect

The observer effect suggests that a situation or phenomenon can change by observing it. For instance, a person may change their behavior if they know they are being observed, such as employees working harder because their boss is watching them on camera. This theory can be applied to manifestation. Focusing on your goals can impact their outcome. You can change your reality by giving all your attention to your goals.

Alternate Realities

Alternate realities are the belief that a parallel universe exists similar to this one. You can use this theory in manifestation by believing there are different versions of reality and infinite possibilities of outcomes. Visualize yourself in any of those realities, living your life as if your desires are manifested.

The Power of Belief and Emotional Alignment

Manifestation won't work without belief. You will never achieve your goals if you don't believe in yourself and the universe. Belief is what separates manifestation from wishful thinking. Wishful thinking isn't always realistic. You simply close your eyes and daydream of different scenarios or make a wish without any emotional attachment. For instance, you can wish to become a famous singer and imagine yourself singing on stage and having fans fawning over you. It is fun to think about, but you don't believe it will happen and don't take any action to make it a reality.

Belief makes your manifestation powerful and effective. You know what you want will become a reality, and you are willing to act and work hard to achieve your goals. You are confident and trust that the universe is on your side.

Emotional alignment is also significant. Your emotions determine your vibrational frequencies. Make sure your emotions are positive and align them with your intentions to amplify your manifestation.

Practical Instructions

Energy Check

Make it a habit every day to evaluate your emotional and vibrational state. Pause what you are doing, close your eyes, and assess how you feel. If you are experiencing negative thoughts and emotions, shift your focus toward a more positive frequency. You can watch a funny video, spend time with a loved one, play with your pet, read a book, listen to music, visualize a peaceful and happy scenario, or do anything to improve your mood.

The life you are dreaming of can be a few affirmations away. Manifestation is a powerful tool that can help make your dreams a reality. While some skeptics may find it unrealistic or impractical, various psychologists have found it effective. Manifestation alters your brain through intention and positive thinking. You will start to believe in yourself and your abilities. Instead of thinking the world is against you, you will believe that the universe is working with you to bring you closer to the life you have always wanted.

Chapter 2: Shaping Your Manifestation Mindset

Having a positive mindset is crucial for successful manifestation. However, this can be challenging for some people. You may struggle with maintaining a positive attitude if you usually face setbacks in life. Limiting beliefs can make you believe that your situation will never improve. Low self-esteem and negative past experiences can make you doubt your abilities. However, you shouldn't give in to negative thinking. You should change your thought pattern and believe in yourself and the universe.

Having a positive mindset is crucial for successful manifestation.³

This chapter explains the role of mindset in manifestation, provides strategies for challenging limiting beliefs, and explores how to cultivate emotional alignment and build resilience.

The Role of Mindset in Manifestation

A mindset is the attitude, thoughts, and beliefs that shape your perception and worldview. It impacts every aspect of your life, including behavior, emotions, and thoughts. A positive mindset is the foundation for manifestation practices. It fuels your intention, encourages you to believe in your abilities, and motivates you to follow your dreams.

There are two types of mindsets: a growth mindset and a fixed mindset. Psychologist Dr. Carol Dweck explains that people with a fixed mindset believe their characters and abilities, such as creativity, intelligence, and strength, are static. They don't believe in growing or changing, which can prevent them from unlocking their true potential. A fixed mindset is usually the result of low self-esteem or poor upbringing.

For instance, a physically weak person with a fixed mindset wishes they were strong. Their friends tell them this can be achieved by working out and eating healthily. However, they believe they are destined to spend their life with limited physical abilities and don't do anything to strengthen their bodies.

These individuals give up when they fail or face setbacks because they believe change and growth aren't possible.

On the other hand, people with a growth mindset constantly work on growing, evolving, and improving their skills. These individuals thrive on challenges and don't let their failures define them. They trust their abilities and see mistakes as opportunities for learning and evolving. They don't allow their emotions or past mistakes to impact their positive attitude. Their growth mindset motivates them to follow their passion and overcome obstacles.

The outcome of your manifestation depends on your mindset. You can set intentions, repeat affirmations, and practice visualization for months, but you won't see any results if you have a fixed or negative mindset. Your thoughts impact your emotions, your emotions influence your behavior and actions, and your actions determine the outcome of your manifestation.

A growth mindset allows you to visualize your goals and repeat affirmations confidently. It pushes you to be more resilient, positive, and focused. You learn to become optimistic and envision yourself growing and succeeding. A growth mindset allows you to align your energy with your desire and prevents negative thoughts and emotions from deterring you.

Manifestation begins in the mind. You won't be able to practice visualization or manifest your desires if you can't picture yourself as happy, accomplished, and successful. Your beliefs and attitude can either attract or repel your goals.

Manifestation focuses on your beliefs in yourself and the universe. Your positive attitude and strong beliefs will amplify your manifestation, as you will send high frequencies to the universe, allowing you to manifest and attract everything you want. Negative beliefs and attitudes release low frequencies. You will be sending out self-doubt and negative thoughts, which will repel what you desire.

Identifying Limiting Beliefs

Limiting beliefs are negative thoughts you believe to be true. They can discourage you from pursuing your goals or trusting in your abilities. These beliefs could be about money, ideas, world issues, your job, or others' jobs. For instance, if you think money is the root of all evil or will never bring you happiness, you will not pursue high-paying jobs or ask for a raise.

Limiting beliefs can hold you back and prevent you from seizing opportunities, getting out of your comfort zone, forming healthy relationships, and changing your life. These beliefs can act as a defense mechanism to protect you from disappointments. For instance, you may stop believing in love if a loved one breaks your heart to protect yourself from further pain.

Various common limiting beliefs prevent successful manifestation. Identifying and challenging these beliefs is key to unlocking one's manifesting potential.

"I Can't Do This"

How many times have you told yourself that you can't do something? For example, you have a job interview and keep saying you are so nervous that you don't think you can do this. Or you want to get fit but don't believe you can lose weight. Do you think you will achieve any of your goals with this defeated mindset?

This belief stems from your inner critic, who makes you question your abilities. It is one of people's most common negative thoughts, discouraging them from taking chances or going after what they want.

Believe in yourself and your abilities to overcome this belief. Push through moments of self-doubt and say, "I can do this" or "I am capable of achieving my goals" instead of "I can't" each time you face a difficulty.

"I Am Not Worthy of Love"

Suppose your parents are abusive or neglectful, or you are a victim of a toxic relationship. In that case, you will believe that you aren't worthy of love. This belief will ruin your relationships. You will push people away and will struggle with trusting others. You may also suffer from low self-esteem as a result of these thoughts and end up in unhealthy relationships because you don't think you deserve better.

Practice self-compassion and forgive yourself for your past mistakes. You should also consider therapy to learn to love yourself and invite happy and healthy relationships.

"I Don't Deserve This"

Say you finished a big project, and your boss praised you for a job well done. However, deep down, you don't think you deserve this appreciation. You don't feel that you have done anything special; anyone in your place would have probably done a better job. While some may mistake you for being humble, this belief stems from feelings of unworthiness and insecurity.

Keep a journal of your accomplishments as a reminder that you deserve happiness, love, and success.

"I Am Not Ready"

Say your coworker tells you that you deserve a promotion and should talk to your boss about it. Still, you don't think you are ready for the responsibility. You have probably had this thought whenever you think of chasing a goal or getting out of your comfort zone. You keep procrastinating until you feel ready.

Feeling ready is a state of mind, not a fact. Most people who pursue their dreams never feel ready, but they do it anyway.

This belief stems from fear of failure and insecurity. It has nothing to do with being ready. You are just afraid of trying and failing.

Don't wait until you are completely ready and start living your life. Take small steps and figure things out as you go.

"This Is Difficult"

How often have you given up before finishing a task because it was difficult? Nothing in life comes easily, and hard work is necessary to achieve your goals. No one would accomplish anything if people gave up every time they faced difficulties.

When you feel that something is hard, remember all the times you succeeded and the great abilities that have gotten you where you are.

"I Can't Change" Or "Thing Don't Change"

Say your partner says you need to be more trustworthy because your lack of trust hurts your relationship. However, you tell them that this is who you are and you won't change. This mindset can impact every area of your life. Perhaps you have been in an unfulfilling job or an unhealthy relationship but can't take any steps to improve the situation because you believe you are stuck and things will never change. This belief can result in a static existence where you don't attempt to improve or grow.

Everyone has the power and ability to change and grow. Start making small changes, and you will soon notice their positive impact on your life.

"I Don't Have Time"

Say your doctor tells you that you must change your lifestyle and start eating healthily and exercising. You tell them you don't have time to work out or make healthy meals (a common belief among people with full-time jobs and families). As a result, you don't live your life to the fullest and miss out on many opportunities.

Time is the one thing people have in abundance. However, they struggle with managing it. Instead of saying, "I don't have time," say, "I will make time." Find out if you waste any time throughout the day, and make a schedule that allows you to focus on yourself and practice self-care.

"I Don't Know How to..."

How often have you used a statement that begins with, "I don't know how to."

- "I don't know how to make friends."
- "I don't know how to make a relationship work."
- "I don't know how to be happy."

Everyone goes through moments of self-doubt. They may question their skills, relationships, or future. Perhaps you believe that you don't know how to be a good parent even though you want children or how to commit to a full-time job. It is also normal to have bad days when you think you won't find happiness. However, if these thoughts are constant and impact every aspect of your life, they become limiting beliefs that hold you back in life. These thoughts aren't fixed and can be changed with therapy or self-help books.

"I Am Not Good At"

Everyone has weaknesses, and no one is good at everything. However, that doesn't mean you can't work on yourself and gain new skills. If you keep thinking that you aren't good at something, you will never learn anything new or grow. This mindset can prevent you from advancing in your career, trying new things, or improving any aspect of your life.

There is nothing in this life that you can't learn. Instead of saying. "I am not good at something," say, "I am not good at something yet." Taking classes, reading books, or researching online to gain new skills.

"I Don't Have Enough"

Many people think they don't have enough money, energy, resources, etc. Perhaps you don't think you have enough money to set aside every month or enough energy to exercise daily. This mindset prevents you from taking action and achieving your goals.

If you think you lack certain abilities or resources, find ways to improve your situation. For instance, you can ask a friend who is good with finances to give you tips on how to save money each month. If you know someone who leads a healthy lifestyle, ask them how they make time for exercising.

Other Common Limiting Beliefs

- I am not good enough.
- I am too young or too old (to achieve a specific goal).
- I will never be a good parent.
- I am not talented enough.
- I will never be one of the best (at something).
- I will never be successful.
- I don't have enough experience.
- I am not smart enough.

- No one understands me.
- I can't explain myself.
- No one listens to me.
- I never do anything right.
- If I want something done right, I have to do it myself.
- I am not confident enough.
- Everything has to be perfect.
- I can't trust anyone.
- Everything's my fault.
- No one loves me.
- I will never find love again.
- I hate people.
- Everyone is so stupid.
- I will never achieve my goals.
- I am afraid of failure.
- I don't know what I want.
- I don't fit in.
- I am too fat for this.
- I don't matter.
- No one cares about me.
- I am not good with money.
- I only work for money.
- Money is the root of all evil.
- Money doesn't buy happiness.
- I am a mess.
- It is too late to start working out or practicing self-care.
- I can't get my hopes up because I am always disappointed.
- My friends won't like the real me.
- Finding a good partner is impossible.
- Getting close to others will end in heartbreak.

- Life is hard, and there is nothing I can do about it.
- I don't deserve nice things.
- I just have bad luck.
- My looks prevent me from getting what I want.
- No one is there for me.
- I am not as good as my friends/coworkers/family.
- People will judge me.

Replacing Limiting Beliefs with Empowering Thoughts

You don't have to allow limiting beliefs to control your life. Specific strategies can help you challenge and replace these negative thoughts.

Identify Limiting Beliefs

Identifying limiting beliefs is the first step to challenging and overcoming them. However, you may struggle with recognizing these thoughts because they have been with you for so long that you have normalized them. You need to self-reflect, think of all the thoughts holding you back, and write them down.

Writing down your limiting beliefs also separates you from them. They are no longer your thoughts but words on paper that you can analyze without emotional attachment, giving you an objective view.

Find Their Origin

After recognizing your limiting beliefs, look for their origin. Where did these thoughts come from? What situations trigger them? For instance, you believe that you aren't good enough. Perhaps your parents never made you feel appreciated, pointed out your flaws, destroyed your self-esteem, or made you earn their love. Maybe you have been in an abusive relationship, and your partner manipulated and gaslighted you to feel superior.

You can't overcome limiting beliefs without first understanding their *origins*. This will help you avoid triggering situations or people who make you feel bad about yourself.

Challenge Your Limiting Beliefs

Read the limiting beliefs you wrote out loud to determine which ones are real and which ones are negative thoughts that prevent successful manifestation. Negative thoughts are easily recognized because they aren't based on facts. For instance, you believe that nobody loves you. However, if you assess this belief, you will realize it isn't true. You will find that your friends, family, neighbors, coworkers, etc., love and care about you. Evaluate each belief and find evidence to support its falsehood.

Ask yourself these questions.

- What facts support these beliefs?
- Are these beliefs grounded?
- Have you always had these beliefs? If not, what or who made you feel this way?
- Is there evidence that can contradict these thoughts?
- What would happen if you started thinking the opposite of these beliefs?
- Do these beliefs hold you back or push you forward?

Rephrasing Limiting Beliefs into a Constructive Belief

Don't accept these beliefs as facts or let them ruin your life. Challenge and rephrase these thoughts with helpful and constructive ones. Think of beliefs that boost your self-esteem and improve your life. You can use affirmation to change your thought pattern, such as "I am enough" or "I am strong and capable." Repeat these statements out loud to reassure yourself and replace negative thoughts with positive ones.

You can also reframe these thoughts by contradicting them. For instance, you can change "I don't have what it takes to get promoted" to "I am a hard worker and have the necessary skills to advance in my career." You can also change "I don't have time to exercise and practice self-care" to "I can manage my time to focus on my health."

Take Action

Start implementing your new mindset in every aspect of your life. Challenge and rephrase any limited beliefs you experience throughout the day into positive thoughts. Use statements or affirmations that allow you to create the reality you have always wanted. Once you overcome these beliefs, you can manifest your desires and believe they will become reality.

Benefits of Empowering (Positive) Beliefs

Empowering beliefs can transform your life. They can boost your self-esteem and your mood. These beliefs motivate you to pursue and achieve your goals. They push you to get out of your comfort zone and grow to become the best version of yourself. You will notice the impact of these beliefs when you find inspiration, strength, and positive energy in every area of your life.

Characteristics of Empowering Beliefs

- They motivate you and make you feel secure.
- They push you to take action and change your life.
- They help you reach your full potential.
- They don't hold you back. You will have the courage to take risks, learn new skills, and grow.

Cultivating Emotional Alignment

Aligning your emotions with your intention raises its frequency, infusing your intention with energy and amplifying your manifestation. Emotional alignment connects you with the universe and your authentic self. It provides you with the calmness and clarity required for manifestation. Positive emotions have a high frequency, strengthening your manifestation. They also act as a catalyst for bringing your dreams to reality.

Emotions connect your intentions with your desires. You can establish a vibrational alignment with your goals if you feel joy or gratitude. However, negative feelings, such as fear or doubt, can block manifestation.

How to Cultivate Emotional Alignment?

- **Positive Thinking:** Challenge negative thoughts by reframing them with positive and empowering beliefs. Remove clutter, use incense, and play soft music to create a positive environment at home and work. Surround yourself with positive people who lift you and remind you of what you are capable of and how amazing you are.
- **Emotional Regulation:** Life is filled with stressful situations, and it is easy to get lost in them. You may lose your temper, feel anxious, or get frustrated. Repeating positive affirmations,

meditation, breathing exercises, journaling, and practicing gratitude can help you manage your emotions and facilitate emotional alignment.

- **Setting Clear Intentions:** Recognizing the goals you want to manifest ensures that your thoughts, emotions, and actions align with your intentions.
- **Practicing Mindfulness:** Mindful exercises such as yoga and meditation keep you focused on the present moment and foster alignment.
- **Self-awareness:** Check in with yourself multiple times a day to reflect on your feelings. If you struggle to recognize your emotions, practice meditation or journaling. When you are aware of your emotions, you can easily align them with your intentions and manifest your desires.

Building Self-Trust and Resilience

Manifestation is a journey that can be long and complex. You will be in a rush when you have a goal you want to achieve. You will want the universe to answer you right away. However, you may experience self-doubt if it takes a long time for your desires to manifest. You may think you don't have what it takes to work with the universe to achieve your goals.

Be resilient and treat every challenge as an opportunity.'

However, achieving your goals and manifesting your desires can take a long time – but this doesn't reflect on your skills and abilities. You should never give up on yourself or your goals. Trust that you have what it takes to make your dreams a reality. Keep working hard and trust yourself, the universe, and the manifestation process. The road to success is never easy. You may experience challenges and setbacks – but don't give up on your dreams. Be resilient and treat every challenge as an opportunity to learn and gain new skills. Maintain faith in the journey, even when the results aren't immediate.

Tips on Maintaining Faith in the Manifestation Journey

- Practice mindfulness exercises such as meditation, yoga, and breathing techniques to reduce stress and gain mental clarity. These practices will help you focus on the present moment, making you less worried about the future and remaining patient when your desires take time to manifest.

- Change your perspective. Instead of feeling frustrated that your goals haven't manifested yet, trust in the universe. Understand that it is making you wait for a reason. Keep working hard, learn from your mistakes, and have faith in its timing.

- Perhaps you are doing something blocking your manifestation, such as having negative thoughts, losing faith in the universe, or not being consistent with your manifestation practices. The universe will never abandon you, so evaluate your emotional alignment, intentions, or manifestation practices, make the necessary changes, and try again. Maybe you only depend on manifestation and aren't working to achieve your goals. Make a plan and see what you need to do to help manifest your desires, such as learning new skills, exercising, working more hours, etc.

- Remember, you should always believe that your desires will manifest. Act like your dreams have already come true, even if it takes the universe longer than you hope. Have faith in the manifestation process.

Tips to Build Self-Trust

- Be yourself without worrying about other people's judgment.
- Don't manifest unrealistic goals. They will be impossible to achieve, and you will feel discouraged and lose faith in your abilities.

- Stand by your decisions, and don't question them. Believe that you have the skills and abilities to make the right choices.
- Instead of losing faith in your abilities, strengthen your weaknesses and cultivate new skills.
- Don't listen to your inner critic. The voice behind your negative thoughts wants to destroy your self-esteem. Reframe those thoughts by repeating affirmations or finding evidence to contradict them.
- Practice self-compassion and kindness. Forgive yourself for your mistakes, speak kindly to and about yourself, and don't tolerate disrespect from others.

Tips to Build Resilience

- Find a sense of purpose and only focus on your goals.
- Learn from your mistakes and take responsibility for your actions.
- Resilient people are optimistic. They have faith in themselves and the universe no matter how bad things get, and they maintain a hopeful mindset in the face of adversity.
- Develop problem-solving skills that allow you to fix any issue and prevent you from feeling nervous or stressed.
- Change is the only constant thing in life. Don't fight it and embrace it. Life may take you in different directions, so trust the journey and the universe.
- Resilient individuals don't allow their past mistakes to dictate their behavior. They find healthy coping mechanisms to deal with their mistakes and regrets and leave the past behind.
- They aren't passive individuals. They act to change their lives and make strategic plans for a better future.
- Resilient people don't hesitate to ask for help when they need it. They understand that it takes courage and confidence to reach out to someone when they are struggling.

Practical Instructions

Limiting Beliefs Worksheet

Use this worksheet to identify limiting beliefs, explore their origins, and reframe them as supportive, positive beliefs.

LIMITING BELIEFS	THEIR ORIGINS	POSITIVE BELIEFS

Let go of your limiting beliefs, which hold you back and prevent you from unlocking your manifestation potential. Reframe negative beliefs and replace them with positive thoughts. Align your emotions with your intentions to strengthen your manifestation. Boost your self-esteem and resilience, and believe the universe won't abandon you.

Chapter 3: Creating Your Manifestation Toolkit

Manifestation is an interesting experience that involves multiple practices that can bring your dreams to life. Now that you have learned about its impact on your thoughts and understand how to challenge negative beliefs that can block your intention, you are ready to start manifesting.

This chapter provides various tools that can enhance the manifestation process. You will explore each one and learn about their purposes. You will also find multiple exercises to apply what you learned in this chapter.

The Role of Manifestation Tools

Manifestation tools play a crucial role. They help you determine your goals, make you believe they are attainable, and provide a realistic image of how it feels like to see your desire manifested. These tools are also integrated with practical goal-setting techniques to help you focus your attention and energy on achieving your dreams.

Manifestation tools can also physically represent your intentions, making them more tangible and reinforcing your focus on desired outcomes. For instance, a vision board creates a visual representation of your goals. They are no longer thoughts or images in your head but words and pictures on a wall that you can look at daily for inspiration and motivation.

Introducing Manifestation Tools

Discover various manifestation tools to create a toolkit that you can use to manifest your dreams.

Vision Boards

A vision board, also called an action board, goal board, action board, or mood board, is a collection or collage of visuals such as drawings, quotations, photographs, or pictures from magazines that physically represent your aspirations, dreams, and goals. These images should motivate you to manifest your vision.

You should place your vision board where you can often see it.[5]

Vision boards usually focus on one aspect of your life, such as your career or romantic relationships. You can also use them for your short-term and long-term goals. For instance, you can create a vision board for a trip to Paris next summer to motivate you to save money or to start a business in the next five years.

You should place your vision board where you can often see it, such as on your fridge or bedroom wall. You can also create a digital copy and keep it on your phone.

Some people are skeptical about vision boards. They don't understand how hanging a few pictures on the wall can help them achieve their goals. Vision boards are associated with the law of attraction and visualization. Constantly looking at the physical representation of your goals allows you to align your emotions, thoughts, beliefs, and actions to accomplish them.

According to a 2019 study by the Helen Wills Neuroscience Institute, the brain associates better with visual imagery than any other type of stimuli because they are more memorable. Your brain may struggle to remember your goals if you write them down, but it will store the images collected from vision boards.

In your daily hectic life, it is easy to get distracted and forget about your dreams. However, when you look at your vision board and visualize achieving your dreams, you reinforce your goals subconsciously. Simply, it reminds you of your desires, so you do something small each day to bring yourself closer to them.

Ideas for Vision Boards
- Health goals
- Financial goals
- Career goals
- Relationships goals
- Place you want to visit
- Awards you would like to win
- Spiritual or mental growth
- Personality traits you would like to develop, such as confidence
- Hobbies
- Skills you want to learn
- Lifestyle changes
- Changing your fashion style
- Buying a new home
- New experiences
- An adventure you would like to have

Benefits of Creating a Vision Board
- Enhancing self-reflection
- Giving you a better perspective on your goals
- Reducing stress

- Motivating you to bring your dreams to life
- Clarifying your goals
- Improving your well-being
- Increasing the chances of success

Tips Before Making a Vision Board

- **Define Your Goals:** Self-reflect and decide on the goal you want to manifest.
- **Decide on a Medium:** Choose a medium for your vision board, such as a cork board, magnetic board (to stick it on the fridge), whiteboard, wire board, canvas, wooden board, cardboard, poster board, or foam board. You can also create a vision board on Pinterest, Canva, Google Slides, or PowerPoint.

Crystals

Crystals are solid materials where the molecules are formed in a repeated pattern and come in different sizes, shapes, and colors. They can help you manifest your dreams. Each has unique characteristics, energy signature, vibration, and healing properties that amplify the power of your intentions. You can use them to focus your emotions and thoughts on your desires.

Crystals can help you manifest your dreams.[6]

Each crystal has different characteristics related to manifestation and goals, such as love, success, and abundance. Choose the one you feel drawn to and harness its properties to align your vibrations and frequency with your dreams, opening a pathway to manifest your desires.

Crystals You Can Use for Manifestation

- Citrine for success
- Rose Quartz (love and harmony)
- Amethyst (Guiding your intuition)
- Labradorite (Magic)
- Sodalite (Harmony)
- Moonstone (New beginning)
- Tiger's Eye (Courage)
- Malachite (Transformation and growth)
- Lapis Lazuli (Self-reflection)
- Black Obsidian (Protection)
- Clear Quartz (Amplifies your intentions and other crystals)
- Green Aventurine (Positivity and good luck)

Journals

Writing down your goals and dreams in a journal helps you focus on them. This technique allows you to use your creativity and power of imagination to visualize the life you have always wanted and write it down as a story. For instance, if your goal is to find your soulmate, you can write your love story as if it has already happened. You can also write your intentions, daily reflections, things you are grateful for, and affirmations and positive thoughts associated with your goals.

Guided Meditations

Guided meditation can help you visualize the outcome of your desires and strengthen your brain, giving you the mental stamina to chase your dreams.

Benefits of Guided Meditation:

- Reduces negative thoughts and emotions
- Boosts your creativity
- Makes you more mindful and focused on the present

- Makes you more self-aware
- Reduces symptoms of stress and anxiety
- Helps regulate your emotions
- Provides a sense of calmness, relaxation, and peacefulness

Affirmation Cards/Oracle Cards

Affirmations are positive statements that should be repeated regularly to shift your mindset and reframe negative thoughts. Oracle cards are a deck of creative cards that offer wisdom and messages. They allow you to tap into your intuition to gain clarity. These cards guide every aspect of your life, including family, growth, ancestral healing, career, and love. They can also help you find your path and recognize your goals.

Sound Healing

Sound healing is a type of therapy that uses the vibrations of instruments, music, and other healing sounds to awaken the energy of your body, mind, and spirit and promote relaxation and healing. Sound healing can release negative energy that blocks your manifestation, awakening your intuition to connect you with your goals.

Sound healing can release negative energy.[7]

Digital Apps

Many apps offer guided meditations, sound healing, and affirmations to enhance your manifestation practices. Download them on your phone and practice manifestation anytime and anywhere.

Practical Instructions

Discover how to practice each manifestation technique on your toolkit.

Create a Vision Board
Materials:

- Images that represent your goals, such as words/quotes, pictures from magazines or catalogs, photographs from family albums, sticky notes, bumper stickers, fabric swatches, business cards, drawings, doodles, stickers, postcards, digital images, newspaper clippings, printed words, hand-written words, souvenirs, colorful construction paper, scrapbook paper, cardstock, printed affirmations, posters, or clippings from books
- Ledge shelf or command strips for hanging pictures
- Safety goggles
- Staple gun
- Map pins or straight pins
- A piece of fabric six inches larger than your board
- A piece of Homasote board or foam adhesive squares the same size as the space where you will hang the vision board
- Adhesive tools such as poster putty, adhesive putty, hot glue gun, thumbtacks, washi tape, rubber cement, or glue sticks
- Trims or ribbons
- Ink pads or stamps
- Alphabet stencils
- Hole punch
- Paper trimmer or paper cutter
- Scissors

Instructions:

1. Organize the materials you will use on the board, such as pictures, newspaper clippings, postcards, etc.
2. If you have different goals, divide your board into categories, such as travel, relationships, and career.

3. Arrange the images artistically or randomly, but leave an adequate space between them to avoid cluttering the board. You can also add an image in the center representing an important aspect of your goal. Make sure it is aesthetically pleasing so you would feel happy and relaxed when you look at it.
4. Use large images for your main goals and smaller ones for your less important desires.
5. Place your most inspiring images at eye level or in the center. Arrange the secondary images around the main image or in the corners.
6. Choose a color palette for your board to create visual harmony. Use background color or contrasting hues to make the images stand out.
7. Add the stamps, quotes on colored paper, fabrics, etc. Layer the images in a visually appealing way. Keep your vision board exciting by playing with different layout options until you find one that feels right.
8. After you finish the layout, secure the items with glue, clips, or pins. If you plan to adjust the board in the future, avoid using glue because it's permanent.
9. Place your vision board in an accessible place where you can easily see it, such as your nightstand, across from your bed, on the back of your front door, in your home office, on your mirror, an altar, your fridge, or an empty wall in the kitchen.
10. Once you achieve your goals, remove the images and add different ones representing a new desire.
11. Place images of your goals in a box or a scrapbook to remind yourself of your capabilities and victories.

Crystal Programming for Manifestation
Instructions:
1. Choose a crystal that aligns with your intentions. Use more than one crystal if you have multiple goals.
2. Cleanse your crystal with water or selenite, or smudge it with palo santo or sage.
3. Focus on the goal you want to manifest. Hold your crystal close and visualize the goal as if it has already happened. Repeat your intention in your mind or out loud.

4. Charge your crystal by placing it under the moonlight or sunlight for several hours to strengthen its effectiveness and increase its energy.
5. Keep the crystal with you at all times. You can wear it as a necklace or put it in your wallet or pocket. Repeat your intention each time you touch the crystal.
6. Meditate with the crystal every day, repeating your intentions to amplify your manifestation and strengthen your relationship with it.
7. Align your intentions with your actions and work on achieving your goals.

Crystal Grid

A crystal grid can help you channel joy, inspiration, courage, and energy and cleanse you from any spiritual or physical issues. It arranges various crystals in a specific pattern to amplify their energy.

Instructions:
1. Define your intention.
2. Choose the grid you want to use. You will find various patterns online.
3. Write your intention on a piece of paper or use a picture that represents your goal.
4. Choose a crystal to be the focus stone of your grid. It should bring energy into the grid that aligns with your goal.
5. Choose desired stones to place them on the grid's edge to bring harmony and energy.
6. Cleanse and charge the crystals with the previous instructions.
7. Choose a location for your grid. For instance, if you want to advance in your career, leave the grid at your office. Place it near a window, as the crystals need sunlight.
8. After you put the grid in the chosen area, place the crystals on it.
9. Focus on your intention and feel your energy flowing in each crystal.
10. Activate your crystal grid by visualizing universal energy flowing through your focal crystal. Imagine you are tracing the grid's outline to connect the crystals. Follow the pattern with your mind or visualize you are tracing it with your finger.

11. After you finish outlining, repeat your intention and visualize your goal. Make sure your visualization is vivid and engages all your senses.
12. After activating the grid, leave it in its place until your desire is manifested. However, crystals absorb the energy surrounding them. Cleanse them occasionally with sage to release negative energy, or their powers will be blocked.

Manifestation Journaling

Tips for Manifestation Journaling

- Choose whether you want to write in a regular or digital journal.
- Assign time for journaling and incorporate it into your daily routine.
- Find a calm and relaxing room with no distractions to focus on your writing.
- Write, doodle, or draw your visualizations.
- You can add images to personalize your journal.

Prompts to Clarify Intentions

1. What do you value most in life?

_____
_____
_____
_____

2. Where do you see yourself in the next five years?

_____
_____
_____
_____

3. What would your life be like now if money wasn't an issue?
_____
_____
_____
_____
_____

4. What do you want to achieve next year?
_____
_____
_____
_____
_____

5. How will your life change if you achieve your goals? How will you feel?
_____
_____
_____
_____
_____

6. What is your passion?
_____
_____
_____
_____
_____

7. What excites you about your goals
_____
_____
_____
_____
_____

8. How will you commit to achieving your goals?

_____
_____
_____
_____

9. What were your childhood dreams?

_____
_____
_____
_____

10. What makes you feel alive?

_____
_____
_____
_____

11. What habits or routines can help you achieve your goals?

_____
_____
_____
_____

12. What skills do you need to achieve your goals?

_____
_____
_____
_____

13. What changes do you need to implement to manifest your desires?

_____
_____
_____
_____
_____

14. What challenges do you think you will face? How will you overcome them?

_____
_____
_____
_____
_____

Express Your Gratitude

Imagine that you have achieved your goals. You are happy and grateful now that all your dreams have come true. Express your gratitude to the universe for helping you manifest your dreams.

_____
_____
_____
_____
_____

Guided Meditation for Abundance

Instructions:
1. Find a quiet and relaxing place with no distractions.
2. Sit with purpose and close your eyes.
3. Take long and deep breaths.
4. Focus on your breathing.
5. Inhale through your nostrils while counting to four, and exhale while counting to four, too.
6. Repeat four times.
7. Feel grateful for each breath you take.

8. Feel your body and mind relaxing.
9. Keep focused on the present.
10. Express gratitude for everything you have, like your career, health, home, partner, family, friends, children, and clothes.
11. What are you grateful for? Who are you grateful for?
12. Be grateful for everything you have and for being here at this moment.
13. Align yourself with a higher vibration to connect your frequency with an abundance mindset.
14. Notice your thoughts and allow yourself to experience different positive thoughts and emotions, such as love, empowerment, appreciation, hopefulness, passion, happiness, joy, enthusiasm, optimism, creativity, and gratitude.
15. If you experience negative thoughts that lower your frequency, practice gratitude and remember all your blessings to raise your vibration.
16. Think of the goals you want to achieve to give yourself hope.
17. Feel the passion, appreciation, empowerment, and abundance.
18. After raising your vibration, ask yourself, "What do you want to manifest?"
19. Experience how it feels to achieve your goals.
20. You need to believe that you will manifest your dreams one day.
21. You need to become what you manifest. Believe that you deserve it.
22. If you desire happiness, feel happy. If you desire abundance, feel the abundance. If you desire love, feel the love.
23. Feel the emotions associated with your goals.
24. You are now in alignment with a high vibrational state. Everything you want is coming to you. Prepare yourself to receive it.
25. Don't think of how this will happen, and trust the universe. Be brave to take steps every day to achieve your goals.

Making Affirmation Cards
Materials:
- Paper
- Pen
- Affirmations
- Scissors
- Crayons, markers, and paint
- Stickers, glue, and glitter

Instructions
1. Write down ten affirmations that are associated with the goal you want to achieve, such as, "I attract love wherever I go, "I am enough," "I am healing," "My body is perfect for me," and "My life is filled with abundance."
2. If you want to create digital cards, find interesting designs for your affirmations deck. Procreate app and website have a great collection.
3. To make DIY cards, write the affirmation on paper.
4. Fold the paper or cut it into a card-sized rectangle.
5. Adorn the cards by adding stickers, glitter, or drawing on them.
6. Shuffle the cards and choose the one you feel connected to without looking.
7. Consider this affirmation a message from the universe.
8. You can choose more than one card if you want.
9. Repeat the affirmations for the rest of the day or week.

Use the same instructions to create Oracle cards, but you must make adjustments.
1. Choose a pattern for the back of the cards and draw them on the paper.
2. Brainstorm themes for your Oracle cards. Write down any ideas that come to mind, such as poetry, quotes, food, people you admire, musicians, book characters, or shapes.
3. Assign a theme to each card.
4. Decorate the cards.

5. Connect with the cards and notice how you feel and think when you hold each card. Perhaps you see an image or a person when you close your eyes. Write down your observations and use them to assign meaning to each card.
6. After you finish, turn them over and pick a card. Reflect on the card's meaning and consider it a message from the universe.

Sound Healing
Instructions:
1. Sit on a comfortable chair or lie down on the bed.
2. Put on your headphones and listen to binaural sounds.
3. Close your eyes and only focus on your breathing.
4. Visualize your desire vividly and experience the feeling of seeing it manifested.
5. Remain in this state for as long as you want.
6. After you finish, take a few deep breaths and open your eyes.

Music and Frequencies
- 963 Hz: Enlightenment
- 852 Hz: Awakens your intuition.
- 741 Hz Helps: Provides clarity.
- 639 Hz: Promotes love, tolerance, and understanding in relationships, creating harmony between you and your loved ones.
- 417 Hz: Removes negative energy and fills you with positivity.
- Binaural Beat: This is an auditory illusion. When you listen to two tones with different frequencies in each ear, your brain creates a third one, the binaural beat. It can be used in meditation to access the unconscious mind, relax, boost energy, and invite positive thoughts.
- Solfeggio Frequencies: Unique sound patterns that improve your physical and mental health and clarity and help you set clear intentions.

Digital Apps

- Headspace
- Calm
- Insight Timer
- Buddhify
- Breathwrk
- Smiling Mind
- Happier
- Portal
- Anxiety Solution
- Superhuman
- Simple Habit
- Aura
- Soaak
- FitMind
- Unplug Meditation
- Waking Up
- Apollo Neuro
- Muse
- The Breathing App
- Declutter the Mind
- Soundly
- Mindwell
- Balance
- Meditopia
- Ten Percent Happier
- Omvana
- The Mindfulness App
- Healthy Minds Program
- Breethe
- Sound Therapy
- Frequency
- Myndstream
- Endel
- Mindbreaks
- OpenEar's SWELL
- Moodsonic
- Sound wellness and biophilia
- I am
- Mantra
- ThinkUp
- Self Love
- Gratitude
- Motivation App
- Self Love
- Vision Board

Manifestation offers various techniques that you can easily incorporate into your daily life. These techniques allow you to recognize your goals and inspire you to work hard. They also have many health benefits, such as reducing stress and keeping you calm. Practice them every day to amplify your intentions, strengthen your manifestation, and guarantee a desired outcome.

Chapter 4: Visualizing the Life You Want

Visualization is one of the most significant and effective manifestation practices. It allows you to imagine your goals and how it feels to achieve them. However, visualization goes beyond daydreaming and wishful thinking. It requires vivid and detailed imagination, which can impact your subconscious, alter your mindset, and make you believe you can make your dreams a reality.

Visualization goes beyond daydreaming and wishful thinking.'

This chapter explores the impact of visualization on the brain and nervous system, the importance of engaging all senses when visualizing, the role of emotional energy, and the significance of visualizing regularly.

The Science and Power of Visualization

Some people are skeptical about visualization because they think it is an impractical technique that only involves imagining different scenarios and expecting them to become real. However, visualization is a complex process. It requires more brain power and activates the motor cortex located in the frontal lobe, which is responsible for controlling, planning, and moving. For instance, if you visualize yourself moving your arm, it activates the same area in your brain responsible for movement.

This process also activates parts of the brain tied to sensory experiences and emotions. When you vividly imagine your goals, you're priming your mind for success by aligning your thoughts, feelings, and actions. You'll feel more energized by new opportunities – and more inclined to pursue them – because you believe they're leading you closer to your vision. That belief builds confidence in your abilities and strengthens your resolve to overcome obstacles. Over time, this mindset will influence how you think, how you feel, and the choices you make each day.

The mirror neurons in your brain are cells that fire when you act or when you see someone performing a similar action. Similarly, visualizing yourself achieving your goals activates the mirror neurons, and you will feel as if you are going through the same experience. For instance, you visualize that you find your soulmate. You will feel the same excitement, strong emotions, and butterflies in your stomach in real life, as if you are in love.

Visualization releases dopamine, which provides the brain with various positive emotions such as motivation, pleasure, and satisfaction. When you visualize that you are accomplished and successful, dopamine activates the reward pathways in the brain. This motivates you to pursue your goals with persistence and high hopes.

This technique also soothes the nervous system, reduces anxiety and stress, and keeps you calm. Imagining relaxing situations or peaceful images, such as a beautiful forest or a beach, regulates the release of the cortisol hormone associated with stress and activates the brain's relaxation response. This state of mind increases resilience and inner peace.

Visualizing your goals can also reduce anxiety. Imagining yourself accomplishing everything you set your mind to enhance your emotional well-being. You will also start focusing on the joyful image in your brain and what you can do to make it real, distracting you from your worries and making you feel at ease.

It reprograms the subconscious and aligns it with your goals, driving you to work hard and achieve them. It also helps you identify your desires by visualizing vivid and detailed images of what it looks and feels like to be successful. This activity aligns your thoughts, feelings, behavior, and actions with your goals.

Engaging the Senses

You should engage your five senses in visualization exercises to make the experience feel real. Say you visualize walking on the beach and meeting your soulmate. You should imagine the whole experience in detail. Feel the warm sand beneath your feet, smell the air as it brushes on your hair and skin, listen to the sound of waves at a distance, and look around you to see the beautiful blue water and sky. You should also picture what your soulmate looks like, what they are wearing, their mannerisms, smell, smile, etc. Imagine how you feel when you see them. Are you happy, excited, nervous, etc.? You should also picture your interaction, what you say to each other, how they make you feel, etc. Create the whole experience like a movie.

Vivid visualization connects you emotionally with the image you created, making it feel *real,* as if it were happening to you. This emotional connection also activates parts of the brain responsible for action and perception, which drives you to work on your goals. Realistic and detailed visualization that involves engaging all your senses is more effective.

Visualization and Emotional Energy

Emotions amplify visualization by creating a positive feedback loop, drawing you closer to your goals through elevated vibrations and feelings. You also immerse yourself in the process as you engage your five senses, allowing you to experience how it feels to achieve your goals. Emotions add intensity and depth to your visualization, making it realistic.

Once you become emotionally attached to your visualization, it is no longer a mental image but a vivid and personal experience that draws you in and inspires you. The brain senses the connection between these emotions and the image in your head and motivates you to make it real. You will become more focused and determined to succeed.

Your emotional energy will keep you motivated. Passionate people are more likely to commit to their goals, take action, and overcome challenges. Incorporating emotions into visualization transforms them from casual fantasies to desires that drive you to act.

Consistency in Visualization Practice

Consistency is key with all manifestation practices, including visualization. Make visualization part of your daily or weekly routine to amplify your manifestation and strengthen the desired outcome. Envisioning your goals regularly and experiencing what it feels like to live the life of your dreams can be a great motivator. The emotions you feel when visualizing will be addictive, encouraging you to take action to achieve your goals.

Positive emotions also have a high frequency, strengthening your manifestation as you practice visualization.

Benefits of Visualization

- Boosts self-esteem
- Improves well being
- Enhances creativity and problem-solving skills
- Reduces stress
- Motivates you to focus and achieve your goals.

Tips to Practice Visualization Regularly

- **Set Intentions:** Defining your goals before practicing visualization will give you purpose and make the process rewarding.
- **Create a Routine:** Make time for visualization and prioritize it. Remember that thinking that you don't have time to practice self-care is a limiting belief. Visualization only takes 15 to 20 minutes, so you can easily incorporate it into your daily schedule. For instance, you can wake up 15 minutes earlier every day to practice or practice before bed.

- **Ask a Friend for Support:** Share your visualization plan with a family member or a friend. Ask them to hold you accountable if you don't commit to your visualization routine. You can also join a visualization group to interact with like-minded people and feel motivated to keep going.

Practical Instructions

The Mental Movie Technique

Create a "mental movie" of your desired future, where you are the main character achieving your goals. Visualize every detail of this movie and replay it regularly.

Tips

- Identify your goals, be specific, and write them down.
- Create a mental movie of your goal being manifested. Describe in detail how you achieved your goal, how your life has changed, and how you feel after this great accomplishment.
- Visualize while writing, make it vivid, and engage all your senses. Your writing should feel so real that you feel every emotion, listen to the sounds, experience the sights, and smell the air.
- Be very descriptive and write in the present tense.
- You should be relaxed while writing to tap into your subconscious mind and get creative.
- Sit in a quiet room with no distractions. Close your eyes, take a deep breath through your nostrils while counting to four, and exhale through your mouth while counting to eight. Repeat six times. This process will give you the peace of mind and clarity you need before writing.

Senses-Based Visualization

Visualize a specific goal, engaging all senses – sight, sound, touch, taste, and smell – to make the experience as vivid as possible. You can choose any goal you want.

This example is about getting your dream job.

Instructions:
1. Sit in a quiet room with no distractions or lie down.
2. Close your eyes and take a few deep breaths to clear your mind and relax your body.
3. Feel your troubles melt away with every breath.
4. Visualize yourself waking up in the morning to get ready for your first day at work.
5. You hear your alarm go off. You wake up with a smile because you are finally going to do something you are passionate about.
6. You take a shower and feel the warm water on your skin. You have breakfast and drink your coffee. Feel the taste of everything you are having.
7. You leave the house and get into your car. Then, you turn on the radio, and your favorite song starts playing.
8. You can hear the beautiful tune and sing along with every word.
9. You open the window and feel the cool air brush on your hair and skin.
10. You feel your heart pumping out of excitement. You have never been happier because your dream has finally come true.
11. You arrive at work, get in the elevator, and hear its soft music. The doors open, and you walk to your office.
12. You look around you and can't believe where you are. Notice every detail in the office. Look at your desk. What do you have on it? Did you add pictures of your loved ones? Did you put a special item?
13. Look at the view from the window. What do you see?
14. Take a deep breath and smell the air in the office.
15. Sit on your chair and feel the leather on your body.
16. Take a moment to appreciate where you are and what you have accomplished.
17. What do you feel? Do you feel happy, grateful, calm, or excited?
18. Allow yourself to feel at peace that you have now achieved your goal. Feel the relaxation, calmness, and joy wash through you.
19. If you want to smile, smile. If you want to cry tears of joy, cry. Allow yourself to feel your emotions.

20. Immerse yourself in this moment.
21. Stay in this vision for as long as you want.
22. After you finish, express your gratitude to the universe for helping you manifest your desire.
23. Take a few deep breaths and open your eyes.

Creating a Vision Script

Write in detail in your journal as if your goals have already been achieved, then read this "vision script" while visualizing daily.

Example: This vision script is about meeting one's soulmate.

"I can't imagine we have made it a whole year. I still remember the first day we met. We were at my best friend's wedding, and they were one of the guests. My best friend's cousin introduced us because they knew we would be perfect for each other. We shook hands, and I felt something when our hands touched each other for the first time. When we started talking, I knew they were someone special. I still remember what they were wearing and the smell of their perfume.

Although the music was loud, we could still hear each other. We had so much in common and laughed at each other's jokes. They brought me a piece of cake, and I remember the taste of the chocolate on my tongue. It was so strong. Before they left, we exchanged numbers. We went out on our first date two days later. I remember how excited and nervous I was. We laughed so hard until our stomach hurt. I never felt a connection like that in my life. I am grateful to the universe every day for letting our paths cross."

Mirror Visualization

Practice visualization in front of a mirror. Say affirmations aloud while maintaining eye contact, adding an empowering, self-affirming element to visualization.

- I can make a difference in the world.
- I can overcome any challenges that come my way.
- I deserve the best.
- I am grateful for my body.
- I am intelligent, strong, and capable.
- I am worthy of love.
- I am ready to receive love in abundance.

- I am grateful for everything I have.
- I am following my passion.
- I am going to be the best version of myself.
- I am at peace with the things that I can't control.
- I forgive myself for my mistakes.

Multi-Perspective Visualization

Visualize your goal in the first person, then switch to a third-person view (watching yourself achieve the goal), and finally visualize the scene from the perspective of someone else who is supportive, observing you succeed, such as your partner or parents.

Anchoring Visualization with Physical Cues
Instructions:
1. Find a quiet room with no distractions.
2. Sit in a comfortable position and hold a crystal with both hands.
3. Close your eyes and visualize your goal while holding the crystal to act as an anchor.
4. Engage all your senses. What do you see? What do you hear? Is there a distinctive scent that got your attention?
5. Immerse yourself in the experience. Notice how you feel now that you have achieved your goal. Where are you? Who are you talking to? How has your life changed?
6. Keep taking long and deep breaths.
7. How are you feeling? Are you happy, relieved, excited, etc.?
8. Do you want to smile, laugh, or cry tears of joy?
9. Focus on the positive emotions and let them flow through you.
10. Feel them in every part of your being.
11. Notice how you physically feel. How do positive emotions impact your body?
12. Do you have butterflies in your stomach? Are your cheeks flushed? Do you have the urge to smile?
13. Imagine yourself transforming the positive emotions into the crystal.
14. Stay with this feeling for a while.
15. After you finish, take three deep breaths and open your eyes.

16. Use the crystal outside the visualization session to instantly recall that same energy.

Layered Visualization

Break down the visualization into stages. First, visualize only the sensory aspects (sights, sounds, etc.). Then, add emotional responses and overlay empowering beliefs about the goal's achievability. Each session can focus on one layer, creating a rich, detailed vision over time.

First Session Instructions:
1. Find a quiet room with no distractions.
2. Sit in a comfortable position or lie down and close your eyes.
3. Imagine you are walking on the beach. Only focus on the sights and sounds.
4. Look up and watch the beautiful blue skies.
5. Turn your head and watch the blue water and the waves as they move toward the shore. The view is mesmerizing.
6. Listen to the sound of the waves as they move one after the next and the singing of the birds flying above.
7. Feel the warm sand under your feet and the air as it brushes through your hair. Notice the beach's unique smell. Immerse yourself in the experience.
8. Visualize seeing your soulmate walking towards you.
9. Notice how they look in detail. Their smile, body, hair, clothes, etc.
10. They approach you, and you start talking. Notice the sound of their voice, their perfume, and the color of their eyes under the sunlight.
11. Notice how all the sounds around you fade away, and you only hear their voice and the sound of their laughter.

Second Session Instructions:
1. Now, you will focus on your emotional responses.
2. You are standing on the beach with your soulmate.
3. You look into their eyes and feel complete.
4. You have never felt that way before.
5. You are happy and at peace. You are excited about your future together.

6. Feel every emotion you are experiencing.
7. Feel the love and joy filling your heart.
8. Your emotions have become so powerful that you can't help but smile in real life.
9. Focus on this moment and all the positive emotions you are experiencing.

Third Session Instructions:
1. As you stand in front of your soulmate, your emotions overwhelm you.
2. You see your goal finally achieved in front of your eyes and feel what it would be like when it is manifested.
3. You look around, and everything feels real, even the strong emotions in your heart.
4. You believe now more than ever that your goal is attainable and will one day become a reality.
5. Take a few long, deep breaths. Immerse yourself in this moment and the positive mindset you have adopted.
6. Slowly open your eyes. You now know that finding your soulmate is just a matter of time, and you are prepared to make the effort to make it happen.

Future Memory Visualization

Imagine a specific future scene in which you are celebrating your success as if it had already happened. Focus on details such as sounds, sights, and interactions. Recall this "memory" often, treating it as an event that has truly occurred.

Instructions:
1. Find a quiet room with no distractions.
2. Sit in a comfortable piston or lie down.
3. Close your eyes and imagine you have achieved one of your goals, and your loved ones are throwing a party to celebrate you.
4. You are so happy, and you can't believe it.
5. Your loved ones are happy for you.
6. They are applauding and cheering for you.
7. You can see the joy in your parents' eyes as they can't contain their happiness.

8. Your friends are hugging you and feeling overjoyed.
9. You feel their arms around you as they hold you close.
10. You can hear your loved one's laughter and the sound of champagne glasses clinking.
11. You can smell the chocolate cake they brought you. It's your favorite
12. You look around you and can feel everyone's love.
13. Your favorite song starts playing, and you and your friends start dancing.
14. As you dance and have fun, you have become very aware of where you are and what is happening.
15. You have achieved your goal. All these years of hard work, hope, and manifesting have paid off. It has finally happened.
16. Tears of joy are falling from your eyes.
17. This is how it feels like to succeed and achieve your dreams.
18. You are grateful to the universe for everything it has done for you.
19. Take three long and deep breaths and open your eyes.
20. Remember this moment anytime you feel like giving up on your goals or worry that you will never succeed. Believe that this moment will happen. It is just a matter of time.

Visualization is a powerful tool that strengthens your manifestation and transforms your life. It allows you to live the experience of achieving your goals. You see yourself happy, successful, and surrounded by people who support and celebrate you. Visualization will boost your confidence in yourself and the universe and make you believe you can achieve anything you set your mind to with the power of manifestation and hard work.

Chapter 5: Affirmations for Scripting a New Reality

So far, you've learned about the benefits of manifestation and its various methods, including using affirmation cards. You can find many affirmations across multiple sources, but none will be as powerful as the ones you create.

Manifestation and affirmation are highly personal practices. You need to rewrite internal beliefs. The cookie-cutter statements are unlikely to resonate with everyone's beliefs.

This chapter will teach you everything you need to know about affirmations, including how to create effective and personalized ones and the best practices to incorporate them.

The Science and Power of Affirmations

You might be wondering what makes positive affirmations so successful. It's all about the way your brain processes information. Whenever the brain receives new information about the outside world or from the body, this data travels through neural connections. Over time, similar and repeatedly received information leads to new neural pathways in the brain and across the body – creating a physical connection to the repeated information.

Repeating affirmations prompts your brain to create new neural pathways.'

More often than not, your brain will establish pathways for information related to negative outcomes because it's wired this way. It's an ingrained self-preservation mechanism protecting you from "danger" (i.e., everything that causes negative thoughts and feelings). Here is where positive statements come in. Repeating them prompts your brain to create new neural pathways linked to positive experiences and strengthen these. Once it does, your mind won't be focused solely on negative thoughts anymore – and the more you repeat the positive ones, the more your mind will return to them and disregard the negative ones.

According to the self-affirmation theory, positive affirmations are closely associated with the sense of self. People maintain a positive sense of self by reaffirming to themselves what they believe in in positive ways. You become wired to view and reassure yourself as competent and assertive through successes and achievements. This information gets stored in your subconscious. However, when something challenges this belief, the opposite gets stored, and you start to define yourself as inept. Ultimately, this ingrained negative self-definition results in low self-esteem, self-deprecating emotions and thoughts, and an overwhelming sense of incompetence and unworthiness.

Fortunately, there is a great way to subconsciously eliminate negative information and replace it with positive ones. Positive affirmation or self-affirmation can reinforce your core values and strengths (helping you form a positive sense of self) and eliminate everything that may hinder you in developing positive self-evaluation.

Repeating affirmations will give you a serious boost in self-esteem and mood, reduce your stress responses, make it more painless for you to deal with stressful situations, and even help you reach your goals easier. Manifestation is all about making goals and dreams become reality, so having a tool to reinforce your intention to manifest them positively is crucial for success. What could be a more powerful vehicle to empower your manifestation ability than reinforced positive beliefs about yourself, your values, and your competence?

Remember all those new neural pathways that form as a response to your brain learning new information? Each time your brain activates a pathway associated with positive information, two other processes are activated, too. One is linked to emotional regulation. Expressing, controlling, and developing your emotions is vital for living a healthy and fulfilled life. Positive thoughts lead to positive feelings and better control over your emotional landscape.

The more positivity you carry in your thoughts and emotions, the less reactive you'll be to emotional stimuli. And there's more; carrying positivity also improves your ability to control yourself in stressful situations, prompting you to avoid actions that may hinder your goals and prevent you from manifesting your dreams.

The other process is reward processing. Opening the self-regulatory mechanisms causes your brain to flood your system with biochemical rewards that make you feel good about yourself. And that further reinforces the positive sense of self you create with positive affirmations.

Individuals who practice self-affirmations often focus on the goals they want to achieve in the future. As they repeat the affirmative statements, their brain processes a high volume of information about their values and themselves. It reinforces their self-integrity, which causes them to strongly associate affirmative statements with the outcomes they want to manifest. Why? Because their brain keeps rewarding them for the positive stimuli they receive. By contrast, those who don't have positive affirmations in their arsenal will gain fewer rewards because their brain receives fewer positive stimuli and more negative stimuli.

After all, every individual's ultimate goal is to protect their self-integrity. Thoughts and feelings that reinforce values reinforce integrity, shielding against negative influences that threaten development. So, now you know why self-affirmation is so crucial in protecting self-integrity.

Through self-affirmation, you can strengthen your belief that you can adapt to various circumstances (even the most challenging ones), thus reinforcing a positive self-identity. However, self-identity is always in flux, as you can adapt to a broad range of roles, adding many nuances to your identity. This fundamental step helps you learn to define success in different ways, too. Success in reaching goals doesn't always look identical, even for the same individual – let alone for different people.

You may view reaching one goal as a success in one circumstance but aspire to do more in others, causing you to strive to achieve other goals to feel successful. Either way, you're developing a positive and empowered sense of self-identity by seeing yourself adapt and become successful in different circumstances.

A strong sense of self-identity doesn't mean you see yourself as perfect. It means you see yourself handling situations where you rely on your morals and values. Upholding your values while emerging victoriously greatly boosts your confidence and self-identity.

One of the fundamental aspects of positive affirmations is that they help you create reinforcement based on authentic achievements. On one hand, you're affirming achievements that warrant praise because you want to deserve the acknowledgment. Consequently, you'll act in a way that helps you earn it. On the other hand, by reinforcing positive achievements you've reached in the past, you're motivating yourself to strive for them in the future, too.

Whether you use positive affirmation to manifest your goals, aspirations, and interests or reinforce your core values or achievements, it will only work if you keep repeating the phrases over and over again. Why? It's simple. When you repeat information several times, it will ring more truthfully than anything you hear once. So, if you reaffirm positive statements time and time again, your mind will have no choice but to believe they're true.

Do you want to achieve the goals you set for yourself? Practice positive affirmations that reassure you that you'll be able to do it – or better yet, that you've already done it. This approach will give you a more positive outlook on the future, encourage you to take actionable steps to reach your goals and keep that positive reward system in constant motion.

Crafting Effective Affirmations

Want to make your affirmations more effective and powerful? Follow some of the tips below for writing impactful statements.

Start With "I"

"My" also works when referring to a positive quality you want to affirm, but affirmations starting with "I" are crucial for changing your self-perception. They make you the center of the affirmation and bring your attention to yourself, your needs, and your desires.

Always Use the Present Tense

If you think of something as if it has already happened, it will feel right. You'll feel that it will happen because it should happen. So, whenever creating affirmations for yourself, use the present tense to empower them.

For example, instead of saying, "I will work on..." say, "I am choosing to work on..."

When you say the second sentence out loud, you'll feel like it's your reality in the present time, even if it's yet to happen in the future. Yet, it's more likely to happen because you believe it will.

Be Clear and Focused

To make your statements clear and focused, consider what you want to work on. What goals do you want to concentrate on? What area of your life are they related to? What specific aspect can affirmations help you with?

For example, if you're creating affirmations for manifesting your dream job, you can say: "I'm getting closer to obtaining my dream job." It's simple, focused, and effective. Write affirmations for all your goals like this, and you can manifest them with practice.

Keep the Statements Concise

Manifestation through affirmation takes time and practice. You'll need easy-to-remember statements you can whip out and revisit at any time to empower your intention. They should be related to your goals and direct enough that you don't get them mixed up.

Enrich Them with Your Power

Do you know what's the best way to empower your affirmations? By tailoring them to yourself and your unique strengths. Do you find switching from negative thoughts to positive ones challenging but somewhat easier if you can find an alternative? If so, your affirmations should include statements that counter negativity and reinforce positive thinking.

Centering affirmations around your goals is useful, but it isn't enough. Simply focusing on a goal could make you feel that nothing else matters. If you don't reach a goal, it will only make you feel worse afterward, making you reject affirmative statements in the future because you'll think: "What's the point? It didn't work last time either."

Think about what could make it work. Perhaps you'll benefit from tying it to more empathetic and reassuring emotions. For example, instead of saying, "I'm going to work on..." say, "I'm doing my best to work toward..."

Types of Affirmations for Manifestation

You can use various types of affirmations for manifestations, from self-belief affirmations through abundance affirmations to gratitude statements and even specific goal-related affirmations. Here is what they mean and a few examples to inspire you to create your own.

Self Belief Affirmations

Believing in yourself is crucial for manifesting your desires and building the life you want. Self-belief affirmations will make you grateful for everything that has made you who you are and acknowledge that you are worthy of everything you desire. They will also encourage you to recognize your unique qualities, strengths, and weaknesses and prioritize your needs.

Here are a few examples of self-belief affirmations:

"I believe in myself."

"I'm open to exploring and accepting my needs."

"I know my strengths."

"I'm proud of who I am."

"I'm thankful for my strengths, qualities, and skills."

"I choose to be the person who can do anything they dream of."

Abundance Affirmations

These affirmations boost confidence and help you stay even more focused on the goals and positive changes you want to achieve. They also help maintain a positive mindset, making working toward the desired outcome easier. By manifesting what you want in abundance, you can also maximize your power and obtain everything you need to become the version of yourself you want to be.

A few abundance affirmations to inspire you are:

"I can obtain everything I want."

"I attract abundance."

"I can obtain what I need for success in life."

"My abilities are empowering me to create a life abundant in love, happiness, and success."

Gratitude Statements

Have you noticed all the positivity around you? Doing so will promote a more balanced mindset and steer you from manifestation-hindering negativity.

You have many achievements, blessings, strengths, and actions for which you can be thankful. So why not acknowledge them with statements like this:

"I'm grateful for my skills."

"I'm grateful for being able to live the life I do."

"I'm grateful for all the encouraging people I have in my life."

"I'm grateful for what I have achieved so far."

"I'm grateful for reaching all my goals, even the smallest ones."

Specific Goal-Related Affirmations

These affirmations must be tailored to your specific goals. For example, if you want to enhance your creativity, you need statements that make you confident in your creative skills. They need to eradicate doubts that chain your creative energy and prevent you from expressing yourself in a way that resonates with you.

For example:

"I'm unique, and my creativity is unique, too."

"I can express my creativity in many ways."

I don't let my imagination become limited by other people's ideas, beliefs, and suggestions."

"I'm inspired by everything and everyone around me."

Likewise, if you want to create affirmations for clarity, you'll need statements that enhance your focus and self-awareness and bring you insights into your core desires and needs.

For example, you can obtain clarity by saying:

"I see my dreams becoming reality."

"My mind is calm and focused."

"My thoughts are organized."

"I'm focused on making the changes I want."

"My mind is free of limiting thoughts and beliefs."

These are just some examples of goal-specific affirmations. Feel free to craft statements that align with your goals.

Personalized Affirmation Creation

Affirmations work best if they're tailored to your personal desires and needs. To ensure they are best suited for you, you'll need to do a little self-exploration and experiment with different affirmations.

Wondering how to find affirmations that resonate with your goals and needs? Here are a few tips to help you out:

- **Reflect on your core desires.** What do you want to achieve? Is there something you want to improve or obtain? What values do you want to uphold? What is preventing you from achieving your goals? Answering these questions will lead you to the intention on which your affirmations should be based.
- **Think about your negative beliefs.** Are there some thoughts that may be holding you back from fighting for your dreams and goals? Do you tell yourself you'll never reach a specific goal? Or that you don't have what it takes to attain it? By identifying these beliefs, you can craft affirmative statements to counter and replace the negativity with positive thoughts.
- **Raise your awareness of your feelings.** Reflect on challenging situations and notice how they make you feel. What are your thoughts on these feelings? For example, when facing a tough situation you can't conquer right away, do you get frustrated and

think: "I'll never be able to do this?" Understanding how your feelings affect your mindset will provide insight into what positive affirmations will work the best for you. For example, suppose a slightly negative situation and feelings lead you down the path of catastrophizing. In that case, affirmative statements that challenge the "worst-case scenario" you're envisioning will be helpful.

- **Switch to the positives.** List some positive attributes once you've identified negative thoughts and emotions that may hinder you in achieving your goals. Doing this will reinforce the thought that not everything is so negative and that you have the strength to face the challenges. Alternatively, you can enlist desired outcomes associated with your goals or the positive changes you want to bring into your life. How can your positive qualities help you achieve this?

- **Start experimenting.** Write three affirmations that align with your goals based on all the negatives and positives you've identified. Use positive, reassuring language and the present tense. You can, for example, start them like this:

    "I am..."

    "I have..."

    "I choose..."

- **Make sure your statements evoke strong positive emotions and leave no room for negativity.** Write them down or say them out loud daily. Notice how they make you feel and think.

- **Tweak the affirmations.** When formulating and repeating the affirmative statements, pay attention to whether they feel authentic. What's your gut telling you about the affirmations? Do they feel right? Your intuition will guide you toward phrases that evoke inspiration and a sense of empowerment. If they don't feel right, you may need to change the wording to ensure they are suited for your unique journey, and that's all right.

Mirror Affirmations

Saying affirmations in front of a mirror can boost confidence in manifesting your desires. All you need is a mirror and your affirmations, and you can easily incorporate the exercise into your daily routine.

Saying affirmations in front of a mirror can boost confidence.[10]

Instructions:

1. Get into a comfortable seated or standing position in front of a mirror.
2. Take a deep breath and release it slowly.
3. Look into the mirror and make eye contact with yourself. Talking to yourself aloud like this will reinforce your intention and belief.
4. Start with simple affirmations like this:

    "I'm confident and capable."

    "I'm enough."

    "I feel good about myself."

    "I am worthy of my desires."

    "I'm optimistic."

    "I'm in control of my life."

5. Once you state your affirmations, sit or stand in silence for a couple of minutes. Let those statements sink into your mind and body.
6. Take a deep breath, then release it.
7. Once you can confidently repeat the simple statements, you can start gradually incorporating more specific affirmations related to your goals.

Affirmation Scripting

Sometimes, making yourself believe that what you're affirming has already happened is the hardest part, especially at the beginning of your manifestation journey. If you're struggling with this, try affirmation scripting. It requires you to write a paragraph as if your desired outcomes are already a reality, which makes you trust that it will happen. You can describe how you feel and what you've achieved and use positive language in the present tense to make you see what is going to happen.

Even if the reality turns out to be slightly different from what you've written, the process will give you a sense of control over your life. For example, suppose you're manifesting reaching a goal in a certain way, but you reach it in another way. In that case, it will still show you that you had the power to overcome whatever obstacle prevented you from reaching that goal beforehand.

Instructions:

1. Take a pen and paper (or, even better, a journal where you can record your scripts and revisit them to enhance your manifestation/visualization practice).
2. Start describing how your life will look like when you've reached your goal. Use as many details as possible. Where are you? What does this place look like? What do you think being in this place means? Who is with you? How do you feel? What beliefs or values are you sticking to in this new life?
3. You can also use specific language related to your goal. For example, if you're manifesting a financial goal (even if it is to have stable finances), say something like:

    "I'm financially stable."

    "I've reached the financial goals I set for myself."

4. Describe exactly what you want. Once you've written down your desired future, read it over. You can do this right away or set it aside until the next day and then revise it. When revisiting, check that what you've written aligns with your dreams and desires and not someone else's. Do not write anything that someone else would want you to achieve or something that would benefit someone else, even the people closest to you.
5. Later, you can make another script describing how your mindset (and reality) started to shift as you advanced on the manifestation journey. Write how your feelings and thoughts change as you start noticing the power you have in achieving your goals.
6. Write how reclaiming your power, step by step, made it easier to manifest what you've envisioned for yourself.

While mentioning specific dates for reaching your goal (or parts of your goal) is not recommended in the beginning, once you start shifting to an "I will make it happen" mindset, you can add deadlines for your goals because you'll be confident in attaining them.

Another tip is to avoid negative language. Don't write how difficult it will be to obtain your goals because it will only make you think you'll never overcome the obstacles you'll face. Remember, the thoughts and feelings you cultivate during manifestation are what you'll take with you on this journey. If you only take the positive ones, you won't leave room for negativity in your mind and spirit.

Writing about a dream reality in the present tense may seem like wishful thinking, but you'll be astonished at how much you can realistically predict. From the moment you start writing, you're changing your mindset into believing you can make it happen.

As liberating as it may feel to put your dreams into writing, it will be even more fulfilling to see yourself reaching all the goals you've described yourself achieving once you revisit your entries. You can repeat the exercise every couple of months to align your script with new goals and intentions.

Affirmations with Breathing

Effective affirmations include using both the body and mind. By pairing your affirmative statements with deep breathing exercises, you're engaging your entire being in adopting a useful conviction. Choose affirmations that resonate with you and incorporate them into the exercise below.

Instructions:

1. Stand or sit comfortably.
2. Take a deep breath through your nose. As you do, say an affirmation silently in your mind.
3. Hold your breath for 3-4 seconds, letting the statement get infused into your mind just as the air enters the parts of your body. For example, you can say something like:

    "I am attracting success."

4. Then, opening your mouth slightly (as if preparing to blow through a straw), slowly release the air from your lungs. As you do, say something like:

    "I release any doubt."

5. As you inhale again through your nose, repeat the first affirmation. Hold, then repeat the second affirmation as you exhale through your mouth. Continue until you feel that you're making the statements with a sense of conviction.
6. Do this exercise at least once a day.

Chapter 6: The 369 Method and Other Secret Manifestation Formulas

This chapter outlines the concept of manifestation formulas, including the 369 Method, a popular technique revered by Nikola Tesla, and several other unique formulas, such as the 5x5x5 formula or the 2x4 method.

Learning these techniques will enhance your manifestation practice and bring any desire to reality. Throughout the chapter, you'll also receive tips for creating personal manifestation formulas, bringing you one step closer to making manifestation come from the deepest corner of yourself and ensuring a successful result.

Understanding Manifestation Formulas

Before you start learning about specific manifestation formulas, you may be wondering what these formulas are. What makes them so effective and fundamental in manifestations?

Manifestation formulas are techniques relying on the energy of numbers. As the numbers are repeated, the person repeating them aligns their energy with the energy of the numbers. In most cases, success lies not in repeating a certain number or numbers but in using them to enhance the intention to manifest something. In other words, the numbers become key elements in writing, visualizing, and emotionally engaging with goals a person wants to manifest.

The Role of Numbers

Numbers have been linked to spiritual and even religious practices since ancient times. They are wonderful tools for harnessing spiritual wisdom, as they all have unique vibrational frequencies. They can also influence the energy and vibration of everyone and everything they're applied to. From the energies of the universe to the energy of your self-improvement and fulfillment journey, everything operates on vibrational frequencies that can be affected by other frequencies, including numerical ones. Moreover, repeating numbers amplifies their power and reinforces the intention towards which you are channeling them.

Each number is linked to a different energy."

Each number is linked to a different energy, meaning they can be used in personal transformation through goal setting. By understanding which number is linked to which energy, you can align yourself with the ones that best suit your purpose. In other words, it can help you manifest whichever goal you want based on the number linked to the aspect the goal refers to.

Some numbers have a wider range to cover than others, but most have a theme their energy encompasses. Below are the core energies associated with each number and how they can help you manifest your goals and dreams:

1 - Unity: Linked to the origin of everything, number one symbolizes unity and the potential to create anything you want. If you aim to enhance your creativity and craft something unique or express yourself through it, you can use this number to manifest it. It raises self-awareness and makes you feel connected to the energies around you.

2 - Partnership: Embodying balance and harmony, number two is the perfect example of how something with two different sides can work together. It helps opposites work through their differences, so it's great for manifesting goals in a relationship (for example, strengthening trust, communication, etc.) Simultaneously, it can help you find balance within yourself, which can come in handy when your energies are out of balance.

3 - Manifestation: More specifically, the number three is linked to the manifestation of your deepest desires. It can be used in practice when you want to obtain a goal related to your inner self and show what you truly want and need to the outside, physical world.

4 - Stability: Should you need a number to manifest goals related to the material world (for example, finances), number four should be your go-to digit. It helps you build a powerful foundation to set up the pillars of your financial and personal stability. Besides personal development, this number can help you manifest goals for loved ones and community members.

5 - Transformation: Associated with change and progress, number five reminds you of the dynamic nature of life. It shows you that nature evolves – and so can you by facing and persisting through challenges. If your goal is to enhance your adaptability when facing adversities, feel free to use the number five to manifest it.

6 - Love: The number six embodies love and compassion. It is another digit that can bring harmony into your life. Whether you need harmony in the workplace, in relationships, or in creating an environment for spiritual growth, the number six can help you manifest it.

7 - Insight: If you want to raise your awareness and receptiveness to spiritual wisdom, seven might be the perfect number to call on. It inspires self-reflection and can assist in introspective exercises and explorations. It may also help you receive spiritual guidance and elevate your consciousness to a higher level.

8 – Abundance: Associated with spiritual and material abundance and infinite energy, number eight can be useful if you want to manifest goals for long-term prosperity. It may also help if your goals are to establish yourself as an authority and the source of empowerment.

9 – Completion: Embodying fulfillment and completion, number nine signifies the end of the road. If your goal is to grab that spiritual wisdom you see at the end of your journey and never let it go, use number nine to manifest it. Likewise, you can use it to consolidate efforts and practices to empower your road to fulfillment and goal completion.

10 – Renewal: After completion comes rebirth in nature, which the number ten signifies. If you're at a crossroads and want to set goals to find the way to move forward, call on number ten to manifest it. It will show you the new path you need to follow to achieve these and any other goals you may set in the future.

Manifestation Methods and Formulas

There are countless ways to manifest your desires. Below are some of the most popular manifestation techniques and a brief explanation of how they work and their unique benefits.

The 369 Method

Rooted in the principles of the law of attraction and inspired by the work of Nikola Tesla, the 369 methods surely stand out among the manifestation formulas. As in many other manifestation techniques, repeating is key in the 369 method. Writing clear affirmations three times in the morning, six times in the afternoon, and nine times in the evening over 21 days, you gain a structured way to enhance your focus on intention.

So, how does the 369 method work? Nikola Tesla claimed that the numbers three, six, and nine hold a massive significance in how the universe and its energies work. According to this theory, number three signifies the connection to higher energies, creativity, manifestation, and self-expression. It can also be viewed as a trinity of forces linking the body, mind, and spirit. Number six embodies harmony and inner strength. It's the one showing you just how powerful you are and helps you align yourself with the energy you want to manifest. It's one of the most powerful numbers in manifestation and a central tenet of the 369 method. Number nine symbolizes transformation, completing the cycle in which you can release the past and embrace the future. This new beginning number nine shows you is another crucial part of this method.

How do you use the 369 method? You do that by following a consistent routine and the steps below.

Instructions:
1. **Get a pen and a piece of paper.** Tip: Use colored markers or pens, as these will make channeling different emotions and associated energies much easier. It's like color-coding the tools for your manifestation. It's best to do that in a journal, where you can track and revisit your entries to see your progress and remain organized (so you won't skip a day or repeat).
2. **Identify your manifestation.** What goals do you want to achieve? Are you looking for a new job, relationship, spiritual growth, healing, or something else? Take a moment to think about it.
3. **Formulate your first affirmation.** It's best to focus on one affirmation reflecting one goal at a time, especially if you're a beginner. Otherwise, you can mix them up and lose focus on each one. Be specific and use the present tense when creating the affirmation. As always, you want to convey that you've already achieved what you're manifesting. Likewise, ensure that your phrase accurately describes what you want to accomplish. It doesn't have to be a long sentence (after all, you'll be repeating it through the following 21 days). Still, it should be descriptive enough to identify it with a specific goal. Avoid words like can't, won't, don't, etc. Negativity attracts negativity, and what you want is to channel positivity.
4. **Have you formulated your affirmation?** Repeat it aloud or in your mind. Does it sound believable? Is it something you can reasonably accomplish? Does it make you look forward to the future? If so, you've found the affirmation that resonates with you.
5. **Now, repeat the affirmation.** Start in the morning, as soon as you wake up. Take a deep breath and write down your affirmation three times. After each time, take 17 seconds to contemplate what thoughts and emotions the affirmation evokes in you. Your energy is being realigned, so new feelings and thoughts are bound to pop up.

6. **Sit for a few more minutes**, letting the energy of your intention reverberate through you. You've now aligned your mindset to work toward the desired goal throughout the day.
7. **Around midday, sit down again** and write your affirmation six times to reinforce the goal-oriented mindset. It will help you channel more energy into your intention, empowering it to work for you throughout the rest of the day.
8. **Write your affirmation again in the evening**, nine times on this occasion. Do this just before going to bed to solidify your subconscious intent. It will continue working on manifesting your goal while you sleep.
9. **Repeat the affirmation** three times every morning, six times every midday, and nine times every evening for an overall of 21 days.

Visualize what you want to manifest. While this is optional (and you don't have to do it during each repetition), try envisioning yourself living the reality you're trying to manifest. As you write the affirmation and let its energy infuse your intuition, imagine that what you're writing is true. Let yourself feel the emotions you associate with the desired goal. Would reaching it make you feel happy? Fulfilled? More relaxed? Whatever it is, feel it. Allow yourself to immerse in this awesome present-turned-future experience fully.

As you write, visualize, and repeat your affirmation during the 21 days, you may feel inspired to take action and engage in practices that can enhance the exercise. The power of repetition is enormous, but it can still be magnified by taking steps that align with the goal you want to manifest. For example, after writing down your affirmation in the morning or midday, you may feel inspired to decide during the day that'll bring you one step closer to your goal. Whatever choice you're encouraged to make, if it comes from your intuition, take it.

In the 369 method, nothing is coincidental. Even the number of days you repeat the affirmation has a numerological significance. Some numbers have the power to enhance the energy of others, and this is the case with number 21 as well. While some may go for longer periods (for example, 33 days), 21 days are enough for a new pattern to become completely ingrained in the brain - and this is exactly because this number empowers positive mindsets, helping to rewire the brain. During those 21 days, countless new neural pathways can form, and you'll be able to focus on your intention to manifest your goals more and more.

While the method described above instructs for a 21-day practice, you can tweak it and change it to shorter or longer slots depending on your needs and goals.

If you happen to skip a day, don't worry. Unexpected circumstances can occur and cause you to change your schedule. The method isn't about obtaining the perfect score by writing your affirmation on 21 consecutive days. Does it help focus and make you feel fulfilled if you do the 3, 6, and 9 repetitions 21 days in a row? Absolutely. Will you automatically lose focus if you skip a day? Unlikely. It can happen if you skip the second or third day after completing only one, but rarely if you skip a day by the end of the 21 days.

So, what do you do if you skip a day? Acknowledge it, but don't see it as a setback. You had a bump on the road, and now it's time to get back on track. Continue where you left off (this is where writing them in a journal will come in handy), and repeat the affirmation the day after the one you skipped. Focus on staying on track during the rest of the journey.

If you frequently miss days, your focus may be hindered. Consider what this could be. What made you lose focus on your goal? How can you eliminate it? Redirect your focus to what you want to achieve and why; you'll find yourself motivated – and this will help you stay on track.

No matter whether you miss days or can complete the exercise in 21 consecutive days, maintain a positive attitude and don't let anything undermine your effort. Believe in yourself, your energy, and your ability to manifest your intent and goals.

Why must you maintain the feeling or thought evoked by the energy you are trying to manifest for 17 seconds? It's simple. It's how long it takes your intention to fully infuse your manifestation process. Your brain needs 17 seconds to link the thought it's focused on to a certain type of energy. This initial state precipitates the law of attraction at work in the 369 manifestation method. After 17 seconds, you will be aligned with positive energy, and you can start attracting similar, positive energy to yourself.

Besides repeating your affirmation in the 3,6,9 pattern, you should also strive to understand how it will help you reach your goal. You can work this out when formulating your affirmation and revisit it later when you're sitting with it after writing. What thoughts and feelings does it evoke? Do you find analyzing them helpful (use those 17 seconds to ponder on them to your advantage)?

When visualizing the goal you want to manifest, focus on the positives. Unfortunately, the brain is often better at conjuring up images that evoke negative feelings and thoughts. However, you should still do your best to disregard them and bring up only positivity. Once again, you'll attract what's in you and around you. Positive visualization attracts positivity.

Manifestation takes practice and time, so repeat the 21-day cycle when needed. You may not see the result immediately, and this is okay. Just because it doesn't happen right after 21 days doesn't mean it won't happen sometime after, even unexpectedly.

As you write and sit with your affirmations, you may receive insights or have unique ideas to implement on the rest of your manifestation journey. Write these down, too. Not only will this help you remain motivated, but it will also help you track your progress.

While the 369 method is excellent goal-development practice (it encourages focusing on one goal at a time), you can combine it with similar methods to keep track of your goals. For example, you can use it alongside guided imagery, meditation, or vision boards to manifest your goals.

The 5x5x5 Method

The 5x5x5 method relies on repeating an intention for five consecutive days to manifest changes in your life. As short as it seems, this manifestation method can lead to quite a bit of a transformation due to the frequency of the repetition (three times a day). Each time, you must write and channel the affirmations five times. (Alternatively, you can visualize your goals instead of writing the affirmations, creating a mental scene where what you affirm has become a reality.) As you do this during the five days, your subconscious becomes reprogrammed to align your energy with your goals and desires. Repetition is key to manifesting change and aligning yourself with the vibration of what you want to see yourself accomplishing.

Besides the frequency, the numbers used in this method play a crucial role in its success. As it's highly associated with transformation, number five can channel and amplify the energy of change, especially if its energy is channeled several times in a short period.

Repeating the affirmation this frequently across five days prompts your mind to focus on your intent the entire time. You become fully immersed in the energy you want to manifest, making it easier to start viewing the present-tense affirmations as if you're already experiencing the future in which your dreams have become a reality. You remain focused, and your mind starts forming new neural pathways to kickstart forming your new affirmation habit.

Instructions:
1. Dedicate a space for writing and/or reciting your affirmations. It should be quiet at any time of the day (perhaps, for the same reason, the bedroom might work best, but feel free to choose any cozy place you want). You need to be able to think and write without distractions.
2. Start in the morning as soon as possible after waking up, before your mind becomes occupied with daily worries. Light a candle or incense if it helps you focus and channel the energy you want to manifest.
3. Sit in front of your journal and think about a manifestation statement that would work best in the situation. Be specific and use positive language. For example, if you want a new work position, say, "I'm grateful for this rewarding new position."
4. When writing your statement, don't just go through the motions. Think about what makes you feel excited. Are there any words that evoke positive emotions when you hear or read them? If so, include them in your statement. The more heartfelt your affirmations are, the smaller they'll make the divide between your present and desired future.
5. Write a statement five times in a row, stopping for a few moments after each repetition and letting the words resonate with you.
6. Go about your day until midday. Now comes the challenging part – carving out time to write your affirmations another five times during midday. It's best if you already schedule your day around the practice, so you won't have any conflicting or distracting activity planned for either time during the five days.
7. After your midday repetition, continue your day until bedtime.
8. Then, write your affirmations again, five times in a row, taking a short time to align yourself after each repetition as you did during the morning and midday.

9. Repeat writing your affirmations in the next four days as well without skipping. If you skip a repetition, it's best to start over because the momentum you've been building to focus your energy on manifestation has been lost. While you can skip a day without losing focus with longer-lasting formulas, here you can't. Each day and repetition brings you closer to your goal, and each missed one takes you further away.
10. After the fifth day of using the formula, you should feel the emotions and energy associated with what you want to achieve as if you're already experiencing success. The practice creates a deep connection with the feeling of having what you want to manifest, empowering your manifestation ability.

The 5x5x5 manifestation formula builds focus and trust in your intuition. It also bridges practicality with spiritual energy. By connecting with higher vibrational frequencies, you'll quickly rewire your brain. You'll also actively channel your mind and energy to work for you in making your dreams come to life.

However, if you're a beginner, one five-day affirmation exercise likely won't do the trick. You must dedicate time, attention, and focus to manifest your goals. Yet, if you trust the process and continue practicing diligently, you can align your energy with the frequency you want to manifest. From then on, your dreams, desires, and wishes are just a few steps away.

The 2x4 Technique

The last technique in this chapter is perhaps the easiest. It's fairly simple: Write down the affirmation twice a day, four days in a row.

Instructions:
1. Place the journal at your bedside before going to bed.
2. In the morning, grab the journal and write down the affirmation you choose to manifest. Do this as quickly as possible after waking up. Don't leave yourself room to overthink. Just write it down once, take a deep breath, then write it down again.
3. Go about your day as usual.
4. Before going to bed, open your journal again and write down your affirmation two more times.
5. Leave your journal at your bedside again and repeat step 2 the next morning.

6. Repeat the ritual of writing down your affirmation twice in the morning and twice in the evening for four consecutive days.
7. After one four-day cycle, waiting a few days to see whether your manifestation has started working is a good job. If not, repeat the entire 2x4 process.

Creating a Personal Manifestation Formula

Sometimes, you may benefit more from combining elements from several manifestation techniques. Doing so can create a personal manifestation formula perfectly aligned with your values, needs, and goals. For example, the 369 method works best if you focus on one goal at a time but may have set other goals during the same period. Then, you can combine the 369 methods with another one that can help you reach your other goal(s), and you can successfully manifest all of them simultaneously.

Moreover, as manifestation is a personal journey, there is no one-size-fits-all solution. Some may benefit from one method, others from another, and yet you may find that neither works for you on its own.

So, how do you create a personalized manifestation formula? Start by determining what you want to manifest. Think of something that seems like a far-away, intangible dream you want to convert to reality. Let go of self-limiting beliefs and focus on what you want to see yourself achieving. You can even set up checkpoints to verify you're on your way to manifesting your goals. When you reach these points and goals, how do you plan to express your gratitude for your achievement? Consider this before crafting your formula. It can boost your motivation to get as creative as possible and find what resonates most with you.

Once you determine what you want, imagine your vibrational energy when you achieve it. Use your intuition to determine the frequency you desire to manifest. Channel this frequency by tapping into your energy and raising your vibrations to the desired level. Look into numbers and formulas designed to elevate vibrational frequency and use them during your practice.

Continue accessing your feelings and vibrations as you work toward manifesting your goals. After each step you take toward meeting your target, verify whether your energy matches the vibrations of what you want to experience.

Lastly, let go of biases and judgment. You may feel that certain formulas may not work for you because they aren't aligned with what you believe you want. Or, you may have tried them in the past and found that they didn't work. Either way, it's time to let go of past experiences and beliefs. You won't know whether something works in the present until you try it, and this is where the beauty of creating your personalized formula lies. If you think a formula doesn't work because a specific part doesn't align with your belief, why not try substituting that component with one from another formula? You may find that with a new combination, the formula becomes perfectly aligned with what you want, and you can finally start using it to elevate your vibrations to the frequency you want to manifest. You can mix and match until you find what works.

Chapter 7: Quantum Jumping and Reality Shifting

Taking you a step closer to finding and connecting with the version of yourself you want to be, this chapter introduces you to the concept of quantum jumping. Outlining the idea that you can shift into other realities, the chapter explores how you can jump into the future and other versions of yourself and your life where you have reached your goals and dreams. Besides learning how quantum jumping works and what role consciousness plays in it, you'll also receive helpful tips and techniques for attempting quantum jumps.

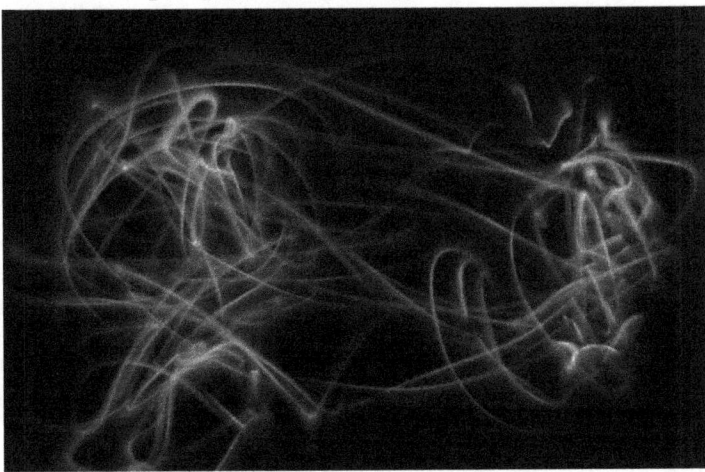

Quantum jumping is a technique that allows a person to mentally shift to another version of themselves.[12]

What Is Quantum Jumping?

Quantum jumping is a technique that allows a person to mentally shift to another version of themselves. It relies on the idea that every person has several versions of themself and can align with any version, one at a time. Just like in quantum physics, the atom can switch between two different states (for example, atoms in gases can shift between liquid and gas states), it is believed that individuals can also change from one state to another. The difference is that people have more than two versions to shift between. However, like the atom, a person can never be in two states simultaneously. If you want to connect with the different states/versions of yourself, you must practice changing from one to another. By doing this, you can harness the wisdom, strength, goal-setting skills, and anything else you need for personal and spiritual development to live a fulfilled life in your current version of yourself.

Understanding Reality Shifting

Quantum jumping involves the practice of shifting consciousness to alternate realities. These realities represent alternate timelines and spaces. How do you change your consciousness from one reality to another? You engage your focus through visualization, meditation, scripting, and other awareness-enhancing practices. The alternate realities represent opportunities for exploring personal growth, harnessing spiritual wisdom, and motivation for working toward goals you see yourself achieving in an alternate reality. It's a subjective experience that allows individuals to find guidance for manifesting desired outcomes.

To attempt reality shifting, you need to be able to immerse yourself in a visual or otherwise consciousness-altering sensory experience. You can obtain this by practicing visualization and intense focus, enhancing your imagination, and being open to experiencing and embracing new emotions. By honing these skills, you can become more susceptible to various states of consciousness, a prerequisite to reality shifting.

Another psychological phenomenon that enables reality shifting is the natural ability to disconnect from certain thoughts and memories and link to others. This allows a person to detach from their present self and shift into a future or alternate version. By engaging in deliberate dissociation, you can become absorbed in alternate realities. Moreover, you lose awareness of your current surroundings, including the worries and limiting beliefs that may hinder you from achieving your goals. With safe practice, you won't lose your sense of self but gain awareness of another self that has achieved your desired outcomes. You also dissociate yourself from the limiting time of your current reality and breach the boundaries of other realities, where everything you dream of is possible.

Lastly, engaging your imagination further improves your ability to shift into any reality you want to explore. By learning how to conjure engaging and awareness-boosting mental images and scenarios, you're immersing yourself in the reality you want to manifest. More importantly, you can make emotional connections between your future or alternate self and your current self, creating empathy and motivation to work toward the goals you have achieved.

It's essential to approach reality shifting with openness. The technique allows you to explore your inner world and find desires and goals you want to align yourself with in other versions of yourself. Yet, simultaneously, it takes practice to safely shift from your current reality to whatever reality you wish to explore.

Consciousness in Quantum Theory

Quantum mechanics, a branch of quantum physics, states that to observe any matter, you must break it down to its simplest form: energy. Matter is seen as a unique version of energy, where movements happen through energy shifts.

According to a similar interpretation, quantum particles exist in multiple states (particle and wave) simultaneously. However, as particles shift from one state to another, scientists only see one state. At another time, the particles may shift to another state and can also be observed in that state. This phenomenon explains why particles give different results at diverse observational times. It all depends on which state is being observed. This is called the observer effect – the principle stating that changes in observation can change how the observed object behaves (or, more precisely, how the observer perceives it).

Consciousness also influences how people perceive something, especially if combined with the observer effect. Physicist Wolfgang Pauli – in collaboration with renowned psychiatrist Carl Jung – studied synchronicity (coincidences in which he believed he could affect the matter around him). He concluded that a person can influence their surroundings by thought. The founder of quantum physics, Max Planck, had similar beliefs, establishing the foundation for studying metaphysical occurrences. One of these occurrences, according to Planck, was that matter is directly derived from consciousness.

Other scientists and psychologists studying quantum mechanics and its relation to metaphysical occurrences have theorized that the way consciousness creates matter can also be tied to the law of attraction. This law states that what you focus on will come into your life because the thoughts you focus on in your consciousness are converted into energy. This energy attracts what you focus on. If you focus on positive thoughts, these will convert into positive energy, which attracts even more positivity. Conversely, if your consciousness is focused on negativity, your thoughts will become negative energy that draws negativity to your life.

Today, quantum physics widely accepts the belief that consciousness is a fundamental process in nature. All beings, including humans, are thought to be able to manipulate matter and energy around them.

Once again, drawing on Max Planck's teachings, it can be established that all matter exists because a force changes its energy or vibrations, as the energy phenomenon became known in popular nomenclature. This force is the power of the individual, which, in humans, is tied to consciousness.

So, how does this discovery in quantum physics and the observer effect tie into the practice of reality shifting? Consider this: If you have the power to manipulate your energy and the energy around you, you can change it to whatever form you want to see it. By altering your consciousness to focus on positivity, you can change the energies to positives – and attract these into your life.

Now, to the best part: You are the observer of energies. You see the energies around you change as you shift your consciousness. Once you start shifting your consciousness, what you see will change, too. You'll start seeing a new reality because you've changed how you observe yourself and the world around you. With practice, you can shift to any reality you wish by focusing your consciousness on it.

The Multiverse and Parallel Realities

The idea that there could be multiple versions of each individual is also tied to string theory, which implies that everything is composed of and held together by small strings. These string particles vibrate at different frequencies, making them unique parts of the individual and their environment. Moreover, these unique particles exist in several dimensions in space. You can see, observe, and experience only one dimension at a time, but there are many others where you and a version of your life exist. This opens up the implication of a multiverse, where the universe you live in is just one of the many that exist in a much larger whole. Each universe in this multiverse has its own laws where energy behaves differently – as do the particles that form people and their environment. In each, your energy and life differ from the one in your current universe. In some, the differences could be greater than you could ever imagine.

According to the multiverse theory, each universe is separated from the other by a membrane and exists in a higher dimensional space. There could be infinite universes, all divided by a membrane that can be crossed through reality shifting. You can visit each because they're a version of your reality. However, you must be aware of the possible changes in energies and vibrational frequencies when shifting to a new reality and version of yourself and your life. This is yet another powerful reason proper preparation and practice are fundamental for safe travel in the multiverse.

Still, if you feel at a crossroads and want to connect with another, more successful, and balanced version of yourself in another parallel universe, you can reach out and align yourself with their energy.

Aligning with a Desired Self

Now that you know that at least one of those realities and versions of yourself has achieved its goals, you may ask yourself, "How do I connect with them? How do I tune into what they're feeling, thinking, and experiencing?"

Visualization plays a massive role in identifying and connecting your successful self. To start visualizing this version of yourself, think about how it might differ from the current one. What does their life look like? What are some similarities between you? Finding something you have in common will make it easier to identify them.

Most people who ever imagine meeting their future self see themselves meeting a completely different person than they are now. However, this would mean you're trying to compare yourself with another person and not a version of yourself. No matter how many changes you implement, parts of you will always remain the same. You'll only be able to identify with a version of yourself if you can glimpse some similarities between you. So, rather than conjuring up an image of a stranger, visualize someone you can see yourself becoming. Alternatively, you can imagine meeting someone who lives the life you desire. The latter will prompt you to start making conscious choices to start living the life of the person you've visualized.

Unfortunately, along with imagining themselves as an action version of their person, most people also struggle with projecting their feelings and thoughts onto their future selves. After all, how would you know how your future self will feel about a positive outcome? If you're like most people, you'll either underestimate or overestimate the magnitude of your feelings in the future. For example, you might think that reaching a specific goal will bring you joy and happiness, and you won't be sad anymore. In reality, you'll still experience sadness because reaching one goal will not make other issues go away. This is another area where imagination will come in handy. You can imagine yourself realizing your goals despite all the hardships you might experience along the way.

By practicing visualization, you're divorcing yourself from the idea of seeing your future self as a stranger. The more you practice visualizing your successful future self, the more you'll believe you'll be that person one day. Moreover, the more connected you feel with your future self, the more motivated you'll be to work toward your goals and make those desired outcomes happen.

So, how do you align yourself with your future self's goals, aspirations, and actions? Here are a few tips:

- **Consider what your future self will value and enjoy.** By identifying values and likes you can relate to, you'll feel more empathetic toward your future self and start taking action to do what works for them. Don't just imagine what your future self has achieved. Think of what they would want to have. Otherwise, you won't be able to relate to them or care about their goals (consequently, you won't care about your goals either).

- **Visualize parts of your future selves live in tiny detail.** For example, instead of envisioning yourself living in your dream home, paint a picture of how this home will look on the inside. How will your future self-arrange their furniture? What art pieces will they appreciate in their home? Then, see your future self walk through the place as you go about your day.

- **Let the emotions come.** As you envision your desired self and outcome, you'll likely experience sudden feelings. Some of these may be negative. For example, you may feel afraid that you won't be able to achieve the desired outcome. Acknowledge this. Intense emotions make the experiences (and the person experiencing them) more relatable.

- **Channel positivity.** When identifying and aligning with your future self, focus on the positive attributes. Show your future self that you have a positive view of them. If you see your future self capable of wonderful feats, it means you're capable of the same – and this positive vision may be why you start believing this.

Quantum Jump Meditation

By manifesting through a quantum jump meditation, you shift from your present reality into a reality where you've achieved the goal you're trying to manifest. The meditation below will help you access the parts of your mind capable of jumping and exploring new realities.

Instructions:

1. Get comfortable and set the intention to relax.
2. Take a few deep, relaxing breaths, enjoying the calm. The more mellow you get, the easier it will be to relax every fiber of your being.
3. Picture yourself on the beach. You're sitting cross-legged on the warm sand and hear the waves crashing at the shore near you.
4. The sun is shining on you, and you feel everything is perfect. Let yourself relax even more.
5. You dip your hand into the sand, and you can feel its texture in your hands. You look ahead and see the clear blue water meeting the beach's golden sand.
6. You're alone, and no one is there to disturb you.

7. Enjoy feeling relaxed and at ease. As you do, imagine yourself getting up and walking along the beach.
8. As you walk, feel the sand beneath your feet. You still hear the waves and birds flying by.
9. Suddenly, you come across a place where the ground splits and see steps leading down. Take them.
10. As you start going down, each step takes you deeper into relaxation, as if you're taking steps into yourself.
11. Notice how easy it is to relax, finding it naturally and breathing with a relaxed rhythm.
12. As you reach the final step, you notice that you've come far from the beach and are now entering darkness.
13. Even though it's dark, it feels good. Notice a small light in front of you. Walk toward it.
14. Now, you notice a pair of golden gates in front of you. Walk toward them, open them, and walk through them.
15. Suddenly, you find yourself in a vibrant place, with birds chirping and everything looking like a dream and not a reality.
16. Ask yourself what your dream is. What would you like it to look like if this was your dream reality?
17. As soon as you start describing your dream, notice how it starts to show up. For example, if you're dreaming about a new job, you're suddenly doing it in this dream reality.
18. As you experience it, consider how it makes you feel. How does it feel to achieve everything you want?
19. Think about how your life would be if you achieved everything. What would you do? Who would be with you? What would you do with them?
20. Enjoy being the person having these experiences. Think about one goal leading you to one of the experiences you enjoyed.
21. Then, imagine yourself achieving that goal. Congratulations, you've just quantum jumped into a reality where you can see yourself reaching your dreams and goals.
22. How do you feel now? Let everything else dissolve so that in this new reality, there is only you.

23. Think about creating the blueprint for making your desired reality come to life. See yourself going to the steps. How would you do it? What steps would you take?

24. With a new blueprint/intention in mind, slowly return to your present reality. Take a deep breath, wiggle your toes, and prepare to work toward your desired outcome.

Future Self Journaling

Have trouble imagining that your future self has reached all their goals? Write to them in a journal. You can write a letter or just a few random thoughts describing how your future self feels, what insights they've gained, and how they experienced the reality in which they've achieved all their goals.

Consider what you know now and the goals you set for yourself. Imagine what your future self will do differently from your present self. Then, tell yourself that you appreciate what they've achieved and want to know how they did it.

As you continue your letter or journal entry, visualize yourself doing something that reflects that you've achieved the desired outcome. Then, see your future self doing something you found useful for realizing your goals. Perhaps you've picked up a new habit or learned a new skill.

Make sure you pay attention to the emotions that pop up as you visualize your future self and are writing the lines to them. Contemplating what your future self is doing, is there anything you can hear, feel, smell, see, or taste that stands out? This will get your creativity flowing and motivate you to work toward the goals your future self has already achieved. It'll also help you set more specific intentions to manifest these goals.

Writing to your future self about your shared goals reinforces your intent to achieve them. You're planting them deep into your subconscious to remain rooted even if you face challenging situations, empowering your intentions even more.

Set a time to write to yourself regularly. Take 30-60 minutes to sit in silence and without disruption and contemplate what you want to say to your future self. Use your favorite writing tools (you can even use different colored ink if this helps enhance your creativity).

Another tip is to write as if you were writing to a friend, describing your achievements. After all, your future self will be just as happy about these achievements because they're theirs, too – just like a good friend would when hearing about your successes.

Determine a precise time and moment of your future life and write to yourself as if everything happened exactly how you wanted it to by this moment. Even as you do this, you may be inspired by new ideas for achieving your goals. If this happens, write these in a separate entry after you write your letter.

As always, use positive, kind language, and don't remind your future self of anything negative. You want to write about what you want to happen – to attract and manifest it. You don't want anything negative to happen, so you shouldn't write about it either.

Don't worry whether everything you write about your future self will be true. Some things may not, and you may experience some pleasant and some not-so-pleasant surprises. The goal is to encourage yourself to manifest and work toward your goals by showing how successful you can be in an alternate future reality.

The Mirror Technique

Mirror exercises are perfect for rehearsing many aspects of spiritual practices, including talking to your future self and seeing just how successful you can be. This exercise is similar to the one from the affirmations chapter, except here, you'll be talking to your future self – the self that has achieved all the goals you set for yourself.

Instructions:
1. Sit or stand in front of a mirror.
2. Visualize your future self looking back on you from the mirror. Create as detailed an image as possible by envisioning how you'll look, what you'll wear, etc.
3. Look deeply into the eyes of your future self and greet them.
4. Tell yourself how great you look and how happy you are focusing on yourself. Congratulations on achieving all your goals and not letting anyone snatch away your dreams.
5. Look at your future self and see how different you are. See how much you've achieved and how hard you've worked to become who you wanted to be.

6. Your future self may tell or show you that although you doubted yourself, you still did it. You were open to new possibilities and used these to lead you toward your goals.
7. Tell your future self about all the goals you've reached. Whether it's a dream job, continuing your education, eliminating toxic people from your life, inviting loving and caring individuals, or anything else, acknowledge that your future self has accomplished this and that you know it.
8. Tell your future self that you are especially proud that they didn't give up when it was hard initially. Eventually, everything will fall into place, and there will be no more insurmountable obstacles on your path.
9. Your future self has everything you want. Let the mirror image motivate you to work toward your goals. Life may throw you a curveball or two before you get there, but you know you'll be able to dodge them and keep thriving. You know this because you saw your future self's confidence and fulfillment when you looked into their eyes.
10. Before you let the image of your future self in the mirror go, tell them that if you ever start questioning yourself, remember your goals and why you set them. Reinforce how proud you are of your future self and tell them you can't wait to walk in their shoes one day.

Shifting with Intention

Proper preparation is crucial for successful quantum jumps, and part of the prep process is setting clear and specific intentions. How do you do this? You start by cultivating the right mindset, beginning with letting go of limiting beliefs and distractions. Consider what helps you focus and what doesn't. By practicing the first and stopping the second, you can formulate and set the right intention for manifesting your goals and dreams after shifting realities without getting sidetracked.

Preparing your mind for intention setting also means opening it for the process. Instead of letting doubt or judgment hinder your intention-setting practice, trust that you'll be able to set the right one. When you learn to set clear intentions, you can elevate your manifestation practice to a whole new level. You'll be opening the gate to a world of new possibilities – the only catch is that you must be open to explore them.

Your intention will help you achieve whatever goal you set for yourself in your quantum jumping practice, but it's also fundamental for safe travel. It takes you to whichever reality you want to explore, as long as you clearly state it in the first place. So, take as much time as necessary to ponder what you desire and where you want to go. Identify a specific goal, write it down, and read it out loud. How does it feel? Does it feel right, like it is what you're meant to do? If it does, you've found the perfect intention and can channel it before your next quantum jump.

Want to learn another trick to set clear intentions and reinforce them? Try visualization. You might need to train your imagination a little to conjure vivid images of the reality you want to manifest, but the result will be worth it. Close your eyes before you start, and take a few relaxing breaths before every visualization attempt. Try to bring up the desired reality, starting with sample images. Do this every morning after waking up and every evening before going to bed. Once you master these images and use them successfully to reinforce your intentions before jumping, move on to more complex scenarios and practice those.

Chapter 8: Daily Manifestation Rituals and Routines

Like any other practice, manifestation works best when incorporated into a regular schedule. This chapter offers morning and evening manifestation rituals you can integrate into your daily and weekly routines and helpful tips on making manifestation a regular part of your life.

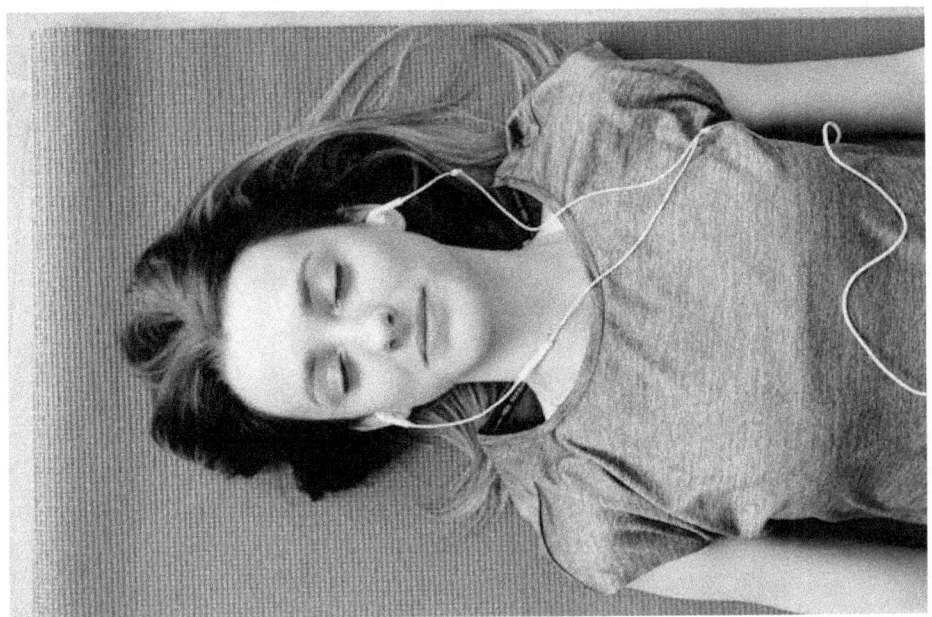

Manifestation works best when incorporated into a regular schedule.[18]

The Role of Routine in Manifestation

Manifestation requires the act of focused intention repeatedly. Consistency is key for strengthening the connection between your desires and goals and their realization. You can't rely on sporadic manifestation efforts if you want to transform your life through effective goal-setting and realization. Why? As you well know, manifestation works through energy channeling. You'll have a much higher chance of reaching your goals by directing your energy toward consistently realizing them.

When you incorporate a practice into your daily routine, you won't have to spend as much time with it. With simple, small steps, manifestation can become as natural as daily chores you've been doing for years, and you'll only have to spend a few minutes every day to achieve this.

Both routines and manifestation have something in common – they work best when tailored to your needs and preferences. By integrating your manifestation into a routine that works for you, you're creating time and space for yourself to work on whatever's important for you. The steps and routine should be something you can realistically do, even on busy days. While it's recommended to start and end your day with a manifestation practice and fit in some minutes in between, too, you should commit to this if you truly think you can. As you'll see shortly below, none of these have to be elaborate practices (although you can make them longer if you wish and have time for it). Even 10 minutes of getting up earlier to do a quick visualization or write a few lines in your journal and reinforce your manifestation with a 10-minute gratitude practice before bedtime can do the trick. The goal is to devise a frame for your consciousness, where you integrate all the positive thoughts and intentions you use to manifest your goals and dreams.

Morning Intentions to Set the Day's Energy

Mornings can be busy, but tuning your mindset toward your manifestation from the start of the day makes you more receptive to opportunities that align with your goals and desires. If you feel you can't spend much time with a manifestation practice after waking up, set your alarm 30 minutes earlier than usual. You'll have more time to evoke a morning intention.

Then, when you wake up and become fully conscious, do a quick, 10-minute meditation affirming your goals. You can combine this with visualization and do a 20-minute meditative visualization, where you close your eyes and imagine yourself achieving your goals. Alternatively, instead of meditation/visualization, you can repeat several positive affirmations after a quick meditative moment when you wake up. To do this, sit up in bed, take a deep breath, and repeat affirmations that align with your goals. It will help you start every day in harmony with what you want to manifest and achieve.

Ending the Day with Gratitude

It's no secret that realizing how many things you can be grateful for can improve your mood. Instead of focusing only on what you don't have or can't do, practicing gratitude teaches you how much you have and can do. This is particularly crucial when trying to manifest your goals. Appreciating the progress you make along the way is a massive confidence booster and a great way to reinforce a positive mindset.

Practicing gratitude boosts vibrational energy, making it fundamental for using the law of attraction to your advantage. Regularly focusing on what you feel thankful for will raise your vibrations, and your mind will project positive energy. Remember, you need positive thoughts and emotions to attract positive outcomes, and feeling grateful will give you exactly that.

By focusing on what you have instead of what you lack, you can shift your perspective to a more positive one. Just as a morning manifestation ritual opens you to new opportunities, so does an evening gratitude practice. Practicing gratitude can enhance your creativity, which you can use to manifest new opportunities, abundance, and success. It can also motivate you to work more diligently toward the goals you're trying to manifest.

Instead of focusing on feeling grateful for the obvious (for example, having positive, inspiring, and helpful individuals in your life, opportunities to grow, or material goods), consider showing appreciation for everything else that contributes to your success. The adversities you face aren't just there to hinder you. They're learning opportunities waiting to be explored and used. So, when they arise, express your gratitude toward them, too, as they'll help you learn how to problem solve and thrive.

Don't use words like but and if when practicing gratitude in the evening. Don't say, "I'm grateful for ... today, but if I could ... tomorrow, it will be much better." Also, only use gratitude statements that express what you're genuinely thankful for. If you don't truly feel grateful for anything, don't say it because it won't come from your heart or help you attract positivity.

To start an evening gratitude practice, set a time for it in the evening (around 30 minutes before going to bed). If you want to write down what you appreciate, take a pen, a piece of paper, or a journal and set it on the bedside table. Go through everything and everyone in your life to see what you feel grateful for. Practice this general appreciation first, and then, you can move on to more goal-specific gratitude statements. Consider the goal and look at what you've achieved already. What steps did you take? What opportunities did you have to work toward the desired outcome? What did you learn from these opportunities?

Reinforcement Through Small Actions

Try integrating other practices between your morning and evening rituals to reinforce your manifestation throughout the day. By taking just a few minutes a day to continue channeling your intentions, you will keep your mind focused on your goals and align with your desires.

These don't have to be monumental actions. It can be as simple as quickly visualizing your goal at the right time. For example, if you want to manifest a better job position, imagine yourself at your new workplace every time you complete a work task at your current job or when you do something to obtain a new job (learn a new skill, improve the old one, take action to educate and prove yourself, etc.).

Likewise, suppose your goal is to heal or improve your life. In that case, you can do a quick mental affirmation to reinforce the positive energy you're trying to attract to realize your goal. Affirmative statements reassuring you that you're healing or have healed (present-tense statements are incredibly powerful in the future) or have improved will help you raise your vibrations and manifest your intentions.

Whatever your goals, what matters is that the small actions you take toward them are consistent. You must repeat them regularly, at least two to three times a week.

Sample Manifestation Routine

Want to know the easiest way to use the law of attraction to manifest your desires? Create a complete manifestation routine. Here are two sample suggestions: one daily and one weekly.

Daily manifestation routine:
1. Start your day with hydration. It gives your metabolism and mindset a boost.
2. Write in your manifestation journal. You can script or record the lessons learned throughout the practice or whatever you want.
3. Clean your space to make room for abundance.
4. As you head toward midday, look at your vision board.
5. Around midday, light a candle or a focus-enhancing incense.
6. Work on raising your vibrations in the afternoon. Listen to meditation sounds or music to raise your vibrations.
7. Practice gratitude in the evening.
8. Let go of negativity and wait for positivity to join you as you prepare to end the day.

Weekly manifestation routine sample:
1. **Monday: Focus on Relaxation** - Start your week with relaxing exercises that help you let go of negativity and focus on positivity. These can include gratitude practices to acknowledge any negativity in your life and/or meditation to embrace your thoughts and feelings before letting them go.

    Once you have acknowledged the negativity, *channel some compassion and kindness toward yourself.*

2. **Tuesday: Enhancing Your Intuition and Creativity** - Now that you've cleared your mind yesterday, you continue relaxing and feeling grateful for everything you can and can do today. After practicing gratitude, bring your awareness to what you want to manifest. If you don't know what it is yet, try visualizing something that aligns with your goals. If you know what you want to manifest, continue your day with visualization and meditative exercises to enhance your focus on the desired outcome. As you do these, continue breathing deeply and relaxing. Depending on whether you've just started your manifestation journey or are

already on your way today, you may also want to look out for signs that what you're manifesting is becoming a reality. Focus on getting in touch with your intuition to encounter the signs in your daily life. If you notice any, take a mental note of them, then record them in your journal in the evening.

3. **Wednesday: Expressing Yourself** – After focusing on what you want to manifest and perhaps identifying signs of progress, turn to kindness and appreciation again today. Practice meditation and deep breathing exercises that help you relax and channel self-compassion. Once you have created a more positive mindset through gratitude, reinforce what you want to manifest by reciting it aloud or in your mind's eye.

4. **Thursday: Finding Emotional Balance and Empowerment** – Today, you concentrate on reinforcing your intention through positive affirmations. It's the ultimate day for balancing out the negativity and positivity and devising a positive mindset. You have channeled the desired outcome and made a connection with it, and now you should repeat it as if it has already happened. Besides affirmative practices, express your appreciation again for what you'll receive as if you've already obtained it. Have a little more time on this day? Incorporate some intuition-enhancing exercises like meditation, journaling, or visualization, too.

5. **Friday: Boosting Your Willpower** – Start with a relaxation practice and techniques focusing on what you want to manifest. Once again, affirm your outcome as if you've already realized it. Afterward, incorporate techniques to concentrate your energy and its power. For example, you could do a visualization exercise in which you imagine your energy outward from your body and feel it empowering your will and intention. Taking in the empowering sensation today will liberate you from any remaining hindering negativity.

6. **Saturday: Empowering Your Imagination** – Start the day with a practice that channels compassion and gratitude. Reinforce your intention to manifest the desired outcome with positive affirmation practices. Then, bring your awareness to your empowering energy and the progress you've already made toward your goal. You can do visualization to bring your awareness and

the desired outcome to focus as if it has already happened. Notice your feelings and thoughts at the end of the day.

7. **Sunday: Completing The Manifestation** – Today, you complete the weekly manifestation process, fully reinforcing the mindset and energy to provide you with the desired outcome. You're bringing positive thoughts, goals, and steps needed to realize them into your consciousness. Repeat all the steps you've completed during the week in today's practices. Channel compassion, acceptance, and gratitude, repeat what you want to manifest and affirm it as it has already happened, embrace the positive emotions and your energy, and visualize how your life will be once you've realized your goals. You don't have to spend the full day doing this. Now that you've already spent the week taking them, five minutes with each step will be enough to fully reinforce your manifestation.

Morning Intention-Setting Ritual

Intention setting can be as engrossing or simplistic as you want it to be. In the morning, perhaps a short technique works best. Here is a simple morning practice: Set an intention for the day, visualize achieving it, and say affirmations. It won't take much time but sets the tone for a productive day.

Instructions:
1. As soon as you wake up, sit or stand comfortably. If you've opened your eyes, close them again.
2. Breathe deeply through your nose and out your mouth, relaxing your shoulders. With each inhale, try to take in a little more air into your lungs, allowing your chest and belly to expand.
3. Soften your jaw and eyelids. After your next inhale, hold your breath for 3 seconds.
4. Imagine your breath flowing in and out of you – as if it were water emanating from its source. Allow it to cleanse your system.
5. Continue breathing as you start focusing on your intention. Nothing else is in your awareness. Just the intent to manifest your goals.
6. As you take your next inhale, visualize yourself achieving your ultimate goal.

7. Take an even bigger breath, soften your body, relax your muscles, and repeat your affirmations.
8. Repeat the previous steps three more times, feeling your intention in your body, knowing it will come to reality.
9. Quickly express your appreciation for the outcome you'll receive as if you've already obtained it.
10. Let your intention infuse your energy. When you're ready, slowly open your eyes. You'll be ready to start the day while your intention works for you, helping you make conscious choices throughout the day toward your goal.

This morning's intention setting works best if you create one intention at a time. Your focus is the strongest in the morning, so use this to your advantage and empower one intention with it. Even if you set many goals, you'll be more likely to realize them if you don't try to channel several intentions simultaneously.

Evening Gratitude Practice

Just like a simple gratitude practice will set the tone in the morning, a brief, reflective exercise in the evening will allow you to review your day and reflect on and express your appreciation for your progress, no matter how small.

Remembering that you have so many little things to be thankful for just before sleep helps your mind focus on the positive experiences even as it processes the day's events and stores them in your subconscious. It will help you sleep better because you won't be distracted by negativity and overly wound up processing information at the end of the day.

Instructions:
1. At bedtime, sit down in a quiet corner and go over your day from when you got up in the morning until you sat down just now.
2. Can you name something you feel grateful for on this day? (Remember to enlist the negative experiences, too!) Avoid generalization, and be specific when considering everything you appreciate.
3. When considering the negatives, consider how you could turn them into positives. For example, if you feel that you couldn't complete something because you needed to help someone, consider what you gained. You had more time to spend with this

person. Perhaps you grew your bond with them so they would become a stronger ally in reaching your goals.
4. Now, consider how many things you feel grateful for are connected to your goals.
5. If you have more than 10 minutes to spend on this gratitude exercise, write what you appreciate on this day in your journal. If not, say them out loud before taking a deep breath and releasing your gratitude into the air. Alternatively, you can record it on your phone and listen to it when you need a reminder of how far you've come in manifesting your goals.
6. Repeat this exercise every night for two weeks. Then, see if you find more things to be grateful for and if you have more appreciation for your progress.

Scripting Journal Routine

Writing about your ideal day (for example, a day in your life from a time when you've achieved your goals) as if you're already living it will reinforce your manifestation and desire every day.

Reinforce your manifestation and desire every day.¹⁴

Instructions:
1. Start in the morning as soon as you wake up. Open up your journal and try to answer the following and similar questions. How would your day look if you woke up on the day you've achieved your goal? What does lying in the bed feel like? Is it quiet around you, or do you hear the noise of the bustling city? What time is it? Look around your bedroom. Is there any detail you can pick up that will tell you about your success? Describe everything in as much detail as possible, and, as always, use the present tense and the first person. However, don't overthink what you're going to write. Just write what comes to mind when answering these questions and describing your ideal day.
2. What do you feel after waking up? What emotions do you carry with you? Are you happy? Do you feel fulfilled? Where do these emotions come from? Do they come from reaching your goal or from what reaching this goal represents to you?
3. Do you do any exercise in the morning? What do you wear? What does the furniture around you look like?
4. If your perfect day includes working at a new position, describe how you go to work, what you wear, who you meet first when you get to work, etc. Describe your workplace in just as much detail as you did your home and bedroom. This applies to any other goal - when it involves an activity in a specific place, describe it and the place in detail.
5. Have fun writing about the different parts of your day. Then, set it aside. You can revisit it later when you're closer to manifesting your goals. You'll gain clarity about where you're headed and the motivation to work toward it.

Visualization Breaks

As eager as you are to manifest your desires or to advance toward your goals, trying to work without breaks will likely hinder your focus rather than empower it. Don't see breaks as a waste of time. Instead, try to view them as opportunities to relax and do a quick visualization. You're reigniting your focus when you take a mental break from everything around you. Do you know why? Your brain is constantly working. While concentrating on working toward your goals, your brain is busy maintaining your focus. It doesn't have time to process and recall memories, activate imagination, or other cognitive functions. By taking a break from focus and doing a quick visualization, you're helping your brain access all its other functions. In turn, you may have new insights or ideas, something you lacked while being overly focused.

Taking mental breaks will also prevent burnout and fatigue and keep your cognitive functions and energy on point. You'll have more (positive) energy to channel toward your intention to manifest your desires.

The best part? You decide when to take a break. However, it is recommended that you take at least a 30-minute break after several hours of hard work (even if it is working toward a goal). Whenever you feel overwhelmed by tasks, worries, or feelings about your ability to reach your goal or how to do it, take a short break to visualize your goal. Visualizing your goal will boost your motivation far more than working relentlessly.

Affirmation Reminders

Affirmations can be challenging to incorporate into a busy schedule. Fortunately, there are countless ways to remind yourself to practice affirmation and keep your mindset channeled toward goal manifestation. With these reminders, you won't have to worry about forgetting to recite affirmations or slacking off while trying to keep your vibrations high and positive.

Nowadays, affirmation reminder apps can be lifesavers. They will remind you to recite your preset affirmation statements at regular intervals. You can either write them down in the app or keep your affirmation cards with you at all times so you can read them whenever the reminder goes off.

Always maintain a positive attitude toward the task and yourself when using affirmation reminders. A reminder going off or affirmations displayed in your app might seem inconvenient on a busy day, but that's why you set them in the first place - to remind you of your goals when you're too busy to do it yourself.

Some apps will offer to write the affirmations for you. Whether you opt for this or write them yourself, ensure they're in the present tense and the first person. Alternatively, if you have only one or two affirmations, you can set them up as a screensaver on your phone, computer, or tablet.

Some may find using apps too impersonal because they lack emotional charge. If you feel this way, record yourself saying the statements in a compassionate but convincing voice. It's guaranteed to reach your heart. Hearing how much you want it and believe in it will make you work even harder toward the goal.

Alternatively, you can also place visual reminders, like sticky notes or vision birds, in a place you frequent regularly, such as your home, workplace, or wherever you want to reach that dream outcome. Write your affirmations in these places or use them as simple reminders to recite them to ensure you won't lose sight of your goal.

Whether you use apps, physical reminders, or any other reminder tool, use them at least once a day to keep them (and your attention) charged with your energy and desire to reach your goals.

Conclusion

As you reach the end of this journey, it's time to reflect on all the knowledge you gained from this book. It's time to put the skills you've developed into practice and put this new-found power to the test. You now understand how to use the art of manifestation to transform your life and bring your deepest desires to life. Whether you're new to the practice or more seasoned, the exercises and techniques provided in this book will help you succeed in this endeavor.

This book helped you understand the connection humans have with the world around them and delved into how your thoughts, intentions, and the universe are interconnected. You should now realize that the words you speak into the universe and the energy you exude to it are potent enough to come to life.

In the previous chapters, you learned about the theory behind manifestation. Also, you learned how to use methods like 369 and quantum jumping to create a life that aligns with your dreams. However, for these techniques to work, you must always keep in mind that your flexibility, ability to embrace change, willingness to take leaps of faith, consistency, and determination are essential.

You should also avoid thinking of manifestation as a destination. It should be an ongoing practice, even if your deepest desire becomes a reality. Manifestation is about enhancing your life and taking control of it. It involves cultivating energies of gratitude, abundance, and opportunities all day, every day. Incorporating the strategies and routines suggested in this book into your daily life can help you establish a positive mindset and attract endless opportunities. You will find that all you need and more are flooding into your life.

The journey of manifestation and developing the skills you need to bring your dreams to life will help you point you toward personal growth and development. You become cognizant of the fact that you're the creator of your reality and that your thoughts and feelings can shape your reality. This is why you must always be mindful of your desires, intentions, and thoughts.

It won't always be easy to stay in the energy and mindset of gratitude and abundance, especially when life becomes testing. You now possess the tools to overcome and rise above these challenges. You can return your focus to your goals and reclaim your power by practicing visualization, journaling, and saying positive affirmations. This will reaffirm your confidence, release self-doubts, and remind you of your ability to manifest your dreams.

Good luck, and may all your dreams come true!

If you enjoyed this book, I'd greatly appreciate a review on Amazon because it helps me to create more books that people want. It would mean a lot to hear from you.

To leave a review:
1. Open your camera app.
2. Point your mobile device at the QR code.
3. The review page will appear in your web browser.

Thanks for your support!

Here's another book by Mari Silva that you might like

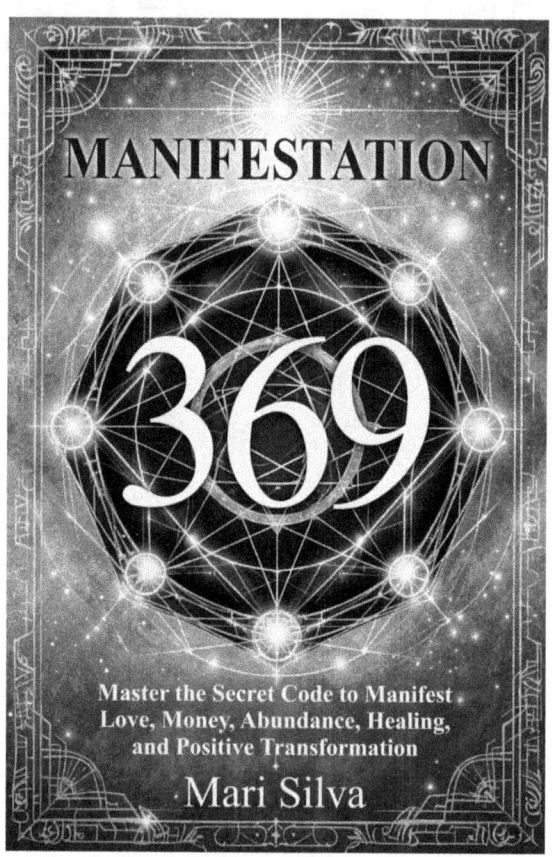

Your Free Gift
(only available for a limited time)

Thanks for getting this book! If you want to learn more about various spirituality topics, then join Mari Silva's community and get a free guided meditation MP3 for awakening your third eye. This guided meditation mp3 is designed to open and strengthen ones third eye so you can experience a higher state of consciousness. Simply visit the link below the image to get started.

https://spiritualityspot.com/meditation

Or, Scan the QR code!

References

13 Common Limiting Beliefs Holding Us Back. (2023). Career Contessa. https://www.careercontessa.com/advice/limiting-beliefs/#examples

5 Best frequency for manifestation. (2024, October 23). Mahakatha.com. https://mahakatha.com/blog/best-frequency-for-manifestation/#439ae22cd46442279f2f22eaf0be9537

6 Steps to Breaking Your Limiting Beliefs. (n.d.). PushFar. https://www.pushfar.com/article/6-steps-to-breaking-your-limiting-beliefs/

Abbadia, J. (2024, May 13). Infinite Possibilities: Understanding The Multiverse Hypothesis. Mind the Graph Blog. https://mindthegraph.com/blog/multiverse-hypothesis/

Aby. (2014, January 10). How to Create a Vision Board. Simplify 101. https://simplify101.com/organizing-blog/create-vision-board/

Admin. (2018, May 31). *Why You Should Use An Affirmation Reminder App*. ThinkUp App. https://thinkup.me/affirmation-reminder/

Bamber, R. (2024, October). THE POWER OF VISUALISATION: A BRAIN-FRIENDLY TOOL FOR GOAL ACHIEVEMENT AND LEADERSHIP. Rachel Bamber. https://www.rachelbamber.com/the-power-of-visualisation-a-brain-friendly-tool-for-goal-achievement-and-leadership/

Bean, L. M. (2017, November 8). *LinkedIn*. Linkedin.com. https://www.linkedin.com/pulse/quantum-leaping-change-your-life-jump-lisa-bean/

Biddulph, R. (2015, May 6). Law of Attraction: Moving into Alignment and Staying There (As Much as Can!) Part 1 – Home. Livelifemadetoorder.com. https://www.livelifemadetoorder.com/blog/law-of-attraction-alignment-part-1/

Bloom, C., & Bloom, L. (2019, September 12). Self-Trust and How to Build It | Psychology Today. Www.psychologytoday.com. https://www.psychologytoday.com/intl/blog/stronger-the-broken-places/201909/self-trust-and-how-build-it

Bonnard, P. (2024, March 14). 60 Limiting Beliefs Examples | Thoughts That Hold You Back. Starchaser-Healing Arts. https://www.starchaser-healingarts.com/60-limiting-beliefs-examples-thoughts-that-hold-you-back/

Borowski, S. (2012, July 16). *Quantum mechanics and the consciousness connection | American Association for the Advancement of Science (AAAS).* Www.aaas.org. https://www.aaas.org/taxonomy/term/10/quantum-mechanics-and-consciousness-connection

braceybee. (2018, October 31). Braceybee. https://www.braceybee.com/blog/law-of-attraction-alignment-before-action

Bradberry, M. (2020, February 6). Living Better Lives Counseling LLC. Living Better Lives Counseling LLC. https://www.livingbetterlivesnwa.com/blog/2020/1/25/diy-affirmation-cards-and-how-to-use-them

Brennan, D. (2021, April 12). What Are Binaural Beats? WebMD. https://www.webmd.com/balance/what-are-binaural-beats

Brown, B. (2021, September 20). Law of Vibration | The 12 Universal Laws of Manifestation. Modern Manifestation. https://www.themodernmanifestation.com/post/law-of-vibration

Capritto, A. (2024, November 17). The Best Meditation Apps for Reducing Stress in 2024. CNET. https://www.cnet.com/health/sleep/best-meditation-apps/#google_vignette

Charlie. (2020, January 29). *Consider writing yourself a letter from the future - www.yourtimetogrow.com.* Www.yourtimetogrow.com. https://yourtimetogrow.com/writing-a-letter-from-the-future/

Cherry, K. (2022, October 6). 10 Ways to build resilience. Verywell Mind. https://www.verywellmind.com/ways-to-become-more-resilient-2795063

Cherry, K. (n.d.). How to Use a Vision Board to Achieve Your Goals. Verywell Mind. https://www.verywellmind.com/how-to-use-a-vision-board-to-achieve-your-goals-7480412#toc-how-to-make-your-own-vision-board

Chuney, A. (2024). *LinkedIn.* Linkedin.com. https://www.linkedin.com/pulse/harmonic-numerology-unlocking-sacred-vibrations-numbers-andrez-chuney-ckx5c/

Cirino, E. (2018, July 19). 6 Ways to Build Trust in Yourself. Healthline. https://www.healthline.com/health/trusting-yourself#bottom-line

Clark, J. (2023, September 6). Does a Parallel Universe Really Exist? HowStuffWorks. https://science.howstuffworks.com/science-vs-myth/everyday-myths/parallel-universe.htm#pt1

Cohen, Y. (2024, November 14). Top 10 Best Meditation Apps in {year}. Www.top10.com; Top10.com. https://www.top10.com/best-lists/best-meditation-apps

Connor-Savarda, B.-N. (2023, April 1). The Science Behind Emotional Energy: Exploring the Vibrations of Our Emotional World | Emotional Intelligence Magazine. EI Magazine. https://www.ei-magazine.com/post/the-science-behind-emotional-energy-exploring-the-vibrations-of-our-emotional-world

Davis, T. (2020). What Is Manifestation? Science-Based Ways to Manifest. Psychology Today. https://www.psychologytoday.com/intl/blog/click-here-for-happiness/202009/what-is-manifestation-science-based-ways-to-manifest

Deniz, F., Nunez-Elizalde, A. O., Huth, A. G., & Gallant, J. L. (2019). The Representation of Semantic Information Across Human Cerebral Cortex During Listening Versus Reading Is Invariant to Stimulus Modality. Journal of Neuroscience, 39(39), 7722–7736. https://doi.org/10.1523/JNEUROSCI.0675-19.2019

Des Marais, S. (2013, October 17). 5 Ways to Trust Yourself More. Psych Central. https://psychcentral.com/relationships/how-to-develop-self-trust#alone-time

Doty, J. R. (2024, May 7). What We Get Wrong About Manifesting. TIME; Time. https://time.com/6975041/manifesting-science-essay/

Dr.Nile. (2024, August 16). *How To Do Quantum Jumping? Meaning and Methods - Goddess.* Goddess Wellbeing for Women. https://www.goddesswomenapp.com/blog/how-to-do-quantum-jumping/#cultivating-the-right-mindset

Ducksters. (2018). Science for Kids: Crystals. Ducksters.com. https://www.ducksters.com/science/crystals.php

Eatough, E. (2023, February 22). What Is The Law Of Attraction And Can You Use It To Change Your Life? Www.betterup.com. https://www.betterup.com/blog/what-is-law-of-attraction

Eyal, N. (2022, September 29). The Surprising Science of "Manifestation." Nir and Far. https://www.nirandfar.com/science-of-manifestation/

Garaca Djurdjevic, M. (2023, March 6). ifa. Ifa.com.au. https://www.ifa.com.au/opinion/32484-the-top-10-self-limiting-beliefs-and-how-to-let-them-go

Goldman, R. (2024, November 19). Affirmations: What They Are and How to Use Them. EverydayHealth.com. https://www.everydayhealth.com/emotional-health/what-are-affirmations/#sample-affirmations

Gottlieb, L. (n.d.). What About the Quantum Physics Observer Effect? Larry Gottlieb Author. https://www.larrygottlieb.com/blog/the-observer-effect

Graham, A. (2024, September 16). *Transform Your Life with the 55x5 Manifestation Method*. Simplyashleygraham.com. https://simplyashleygraham.com/transform-your-life-with-the-55x5-manifestation-method/

Gupta, S. (2023, November 9). Sound Healing for Self-Care. Verywell Mind. https://www.verywellmind.com/sound-healing-for-self-care-8384146

Gupta, S. (2024, September 23). *How to Manifest Your Goals With the 369 Method*. Verywell Mind. https://www.verywellmind.com/manifest-your-goals-with-the-369-method-8620625

Guveya, N. (2023, May 31). The Benefits of the 9 Solfeggio Frequencies. The Pulse Blog. https://ouraring.com/blog/the-benefits-of-the-9-solfeggio-frequencies/?srsltid=AfmBOopbjFW-xj3KaNXwJRbG2oT6bKefrW0e5F4blbgAnxo1JSU3bLLg

Hart, A. (2024). How To Create A Beautiful Oracle Deck In 8 Steps. The Occult Witch. https://theoccultwitch.com/blog/2018/4/17/how-to-create-a-beautiful-oracle-deck-in-8-steps

Hartoonian, Dr. N. (2020, January 6). The Power of Visualization: Imagining Yourself Doing Something Helps You Achieve Your Goal. Rowan Center for Behavioral Medicine. https://www.rowancenterla.com/the-power-of-visualization-imagining-yourself-doing-something-helps-you-achieve-your-goal/

Helmenstine, A. M. (2019). What Is a Crystal? ThoughtCo. https://www.thoughtco.com/what-is-a-crystal-607656

Hermetic Chaos. (2023, June 20). Unlocking Your Potential: The Powerful Five-Step Manifestation Formula. Medium. https://medium.com/@hermeticchaos777/unlocking-your-potential-the-powerful-five-step-manifestation-formula-eb19dd0bfdb5

How can you make your visualizations more vivid and engaging with sensory details? (2023). Linkedin.com. https://www.linkedin.com/advice/0/how-can-you-make-your-visualizations-more

How to be more patient: 7 ways to cultivate patience. (2023, October 18). Calm Blog. https://www.calm.com/blog/how-to-cultivate-patience-in-your-daily-life

Howell, E. (2018, May 10). Parallel Universes: Theories & Evidence. Space.com; Space.com. https://www.space.com/32728-parallel-universes.html

HowStuffWorks. (2024, October). Unlocking the Power of 3, 6, and 9: Exploring the 369 Manifestation Method. HowStuffWorks.

https://science.howstuffworks.com/science-vs-myth/extrasensory-perceptions/369-method.htm#pt2

HowStuffWorks. (2024, October). *Unlocking the Power of 3, 6, and 9: Exploring the 369 Manifestation Method.* HowStuffWorks. https://science.howstuffworks.com/science-vs-myth/extrasensory-perceptions/369-method.htm

Insight Network, Inc. (2024). Insight Timer - #1 Free Meditation App for Sleep, Relax & More. Insighttimer.com. https://insighttimer.com/amandasellers/guided-meditations/manifest-an-abundant-life

Insight Network, Inc. (2024). *Insight Timer - #1 Free Meditation App for Sleep, Relax & More.* Insighttimer.com. https://insighttimer.com/danikadoucet/guided-meditations/morning-ritual-intention-setting-breathwork

Jarvis, C. (2024, May 8). Stanford Neurosurgeon on the Science of Manifestation | Chase Jarvis. Chase Jarvis Blog. https://chasejarvis.com/blog/stanford-neurosurgeon-on-the-science-of-manifestation/

Jean, Erin. (2024). *Quantum Jumping Meditation.* Insighttimer.com. https://insighttimer.com/erinjean/guided-meditations/quantum-jumping-meditation

Jewell, A. (2020, November 11). *Amanda Jewell.* Amanda Jewell. https://theamandajewell.com/blog/manifestation-routine

Justin. (2023, July 24). Here's How I Created an Affirmation Card Deck from Scratch: My Step-by-Step Process - SoCurious. SoCurious. https://socurious.co/heres-how-i-created-an-affirmation-card-deck-from-scratch-my-step-by-step-process/

Kalia, A. (2022, February 3). *"My life completely turned around": is manifesting the key to happiness – or wishful thinking?* The Guardian. https://www.theguardian.com/lifeandstyle/2022/feb/03/my-life-completely-turned-around-is-manifesting-the-key-to-happiness-or-wishful-thinking

Karpaski, D. (2024). LinkedIn. Linkedin.com. https://www.linkedin.com/pulse/easily-achieve-your-goals-mental-movie-method-karpaski-m-a-nbcch/

Kavi B. (2023, July 19). Quantum Entanglement and Parallel Realities: Investigating the Relationship between Entanglement and the Existence of Parallel Worlds. Medium. https://medium.com/@iamkavib/quantum-entanglement-and-parallel-realities-investigating-the-relationship-between-entanglement-379e048524e3

Kehoe, J. (2022, December 26). Are Thoughts Energy? How to Use Them to Influence Reality. Mind Power. https://www.learnmindpower.com/are-thoughts-energy/

King, J. (2015, December 28). Janelle King. Janelle King. https://www.janelleaking.com/blog/mindset-manifestation

Koosis, L. (2024, September 26). *The Science Of Affirmations: The Brain's Response To Positive Thinking*. MentalHealth.com. https://www.mentalhealth.com/tools/science-of-affirmations

Learn the science behind visualization and how it works. (n.d.). EnVision. https://envision.app/visualization/the-science-of-visualization/

LinkedIn Community. (2023, December 6). *Learn how taking breaks can enhance your creativity, productivity, and well-being, and how to plan and take effective breaks for your creative problem-solving*. Linkedin.com. https://www.linkedin.com/advice/0/how-can-taking-breaks-improve-your-creative-speue

Lover, L. (2021, July 13). *Using The Scripting Manifestation Technique To Attract Anything You Want*. One Latte Too Many. https://onelattetoomany.com/using-the-scripting-manifestation-technique-to-attract-anything-you-want/

Makabee, H. (2023, October 30). Replacing Limiting Beliefs with Empowering Beliefs. Effective Software Design. https://effectivesoftwaredesign.com/2023/10/30/replacing-limiting-beliefs-with-empowering-beliefs/

Malu, N. (2022, January 5). It's all about vibrations, man! A theory in which I do believe for life. Our comprehension of the world is not solely about what we glimpse, vocalize, listen to and cogitate. Linkedin.com. https://www.linkedin.com/pulse/vibing-frequency-life-neha-malu-/

Maria. (2024, August 29). Reviewing the Top 9 Affirmation Apps. Vision Board ++. https://www.thevisionboard.app/top-affirmation-apps-iphone/

Mayo Clinic Staff. (2020, October 27). How to Build Resiliency. Mayo Clinic. https://www.mayoclinic.org/tests-procedures/resilience-training/in-depth/resilience/art-20046311

Mayo Clinic. (2023, December 14). Meditation: A simple, fast way to reduce stress. Mayo Clinic. https://www.mayoclinic.org/tests-procedures/meditation/in-depth/meditation/art-20045858

MBA, C. M., Psychologist. (2019, March 4). *Positive Daily Affirmations: Is There Science Behind It?* PositivePsychology.com. https://positivepsychology.com/daily-affirmations/#science

McCormick, A., & Owens, H. (2024, January 31). These 7 Apps Will Deepen Your Meditation Practice. Verywell Mind. https://www.verywellmind.com/best-meditation-apps-4767322

McNally, M. (2024, May 1). *You Are Your Future Self: Learn How to Tune into Who You Want to Be.* Linkedin.com. https://www.linkedin.com/pulse/you-your-future-self-learn-how-tune-who-want-melanie-mcnally-psyd-b6hgc/

Meditation Benefits: Improve your Exercise Goals | Physique 57. (2021, January 5). Physique 57. https://physique57.com/meditation-can-improve-your-fitness-goals-heres-how/

Merritt, R. A. (2024, April 19). Visualization and manifestation have gained significant attention in recent years as powerful tools for personal growth, achieving goals, and creating the life we desire. While techniques and practices vary, there's one crucial element that serves as the explosive force behind these practices: emoti. Linkedin.com. https://www.linkedin.com/pulse/emotion-tnt-visualization-manifestation-raymond-merritt-8nmze/

Michael, E. (2024, September 26). The Science Of Manifestation: The Power Of Positive Thinking - MentalHealth.com. MentalHealth.com. https://www.mentalhealth.com/tools/science-of-manifestation

Mindom. (2024, April 9). Visualization is often viewed as a simple and perhaps even frivolous practice... Linkedin.com. https://www.linkedin.com/pulse/neuroscience-behind-visualization-effect-brain-our-emotions-nmkvf/

Minuto, A. (2024, October 17). The Process of Processing Emotions To Manifest - True Self Manifestation. True Self Manifestation. https://trueselfmanifestation.com/processing-emotions-to-manifest/

Modern Recovery Editorial Team. (n.d.). Visualization: Definition, Benefits & Techniques. Modern Recovery Services. https://modernrecoveryservices.com/wellness/coping/skills/cognitive/visualization/

Morreale, M. (2024, December 1). Manifestation Methods: Can You Really Get Everything You Want? Www.betterup.com. https://www.betterup.com/blog/manifestation-methods

Morreale, M. (2024, December 1). *Manifestation Methods: Can You Really Get Everything You Want?* Www.betterup.com. https://www.betterup.com/blog/manifestation-methods

Mosunmola, Z. (2023, January 24). *The String Theory and The Multiverse.* Medium. https://zainabmosunmola.medium.com/string-theory-and-the-multiverse-e31eceba1495

Neil, S. (2024, August 26). *The Role of Gratitude in Manifestation | Mindset Motive*. Mindset Motive. https://mindsetmotive.com/role-gratitude-manifestation/

Ningthoujam, N. (2024, March 13). *Can the 369 manifestation method make your dreams come true?* Healthshots. https://www.healthshots.com/mind/mental-health/369-manifestation-method/

Novak, J. M. (2024, January 7). 62 Self-Limiting Beliefs that Block Happiness and Success • Believe and Create. Believe and Create. https://believeandcreate.com/62-beliefs-that-limit-your-happiness-and-success/

oneuponedown. (n.d.). Manifestation definition and how to practice it. OneUpOneDown - Women Mentoring. https://oneuponedown.org/blog-post/manifestation-definition-and-how-to-practice-it/

Pavel, I. (2023, June 16). *Simplish*. Simplish. https://simplish.co/blog/types-of-affirmations#affirmations-for-success

Perry, E. (2022, May 25). What Is a Manifestation Journal? A 9-Step Guide to Write Your Dreams. Www.betterup.com. https://www.betterup.com/blog/what-is-a-manifestation-journal

Perry, E. (2023, June 15). 5 steps to create a vision board that does its job. BetterUp. https://www.betterup.com/blog/how-to-create-vision-board

PHR, C. W. (2023, December 18). Welcome to a realm where the laws of physics and the art of manifesting merge in an intriguing dance. In the world of quantum manifestation, we step into a reality where our thoughts, intentions, and desires are entangled in a mysterious web of interconnected possibilities. Linkedin.com. https://www.linkedin.com/pulse/unlocking-mysteries-manifesting-quantum-physics-depth-colin-w-jjxhc/

Porat, A. (2021, July 19). LinkedIn. Linkedin.com. https://www.linkedin.com/pulse/how-harness-power-your-focused-intention-amazing-now-ada-porat-ph-d-/

Primed Mind. (2021, September 26). 14 Benefits of Guided Meditation Backed by Science. Primed Mind: The Best Mindset & Hypnosis App. https://primedmind.com/benefits-of-guided-meditation/

PURI, M., & ROBINSON, D. (2007). Optimism and Economic Choice. Journal of Financial Economics, 86(1), 71–99. https://doi.org/10.1016/j.jfineco.2006.09.003

Ravindran, D. (2024, June 3). The Power of Manifesting: Turning Thoughts into Reality. Medium. https://deepakravindran.medium.com/the-power-of-manifesting-turning-thoughts-into-reality-d6ce5a03e898

Ries, J. (2024, October 9). I'm a Neuroscientist. Here's Why I Believe in the Power of Manifestation. SELF. https://www.self.com/story/neuroscientist-science-behind-manifestation

Rivendell Marketing. (2022, April 19). A Guide to Crystal Grids for Beginners. Rivendell Shop. https://rivendellshop.co.nz/blogs/default-blog/a-guide-to-crystal-grid-for-beginners

Rogers, D. (2024, June 25). Have you ever felt out of sync with yourself, where your emotions, thoughts, and actions seem to pull you in different directions? Linkedin.com. https://www.linkedin.com/pulse/power-alignment-dave-rogers-hztte/

Romano, A. (2024, January 30). Unlock Your Desires: A Guide to Energy Alignment & Manifestation. Affirm Your Reality. https://affirmyourreality.com/what-is-the-science-of-energy-alignment-and-manifestation/

Ross, M. (2024, July 9). What Is Manifestation, and Does It Actually Work? We Asked Mental Health Experts. @Onepeloton; Peloton Interactive. https://www.onepeloton.com/blog/what-is-manifesting/

Ryan, T. (2021, June 22). Binaural Beats for Sleep. Sleep Foundation. https://www.sleepfoundation.org/noise-and-sleep/binaural-beats

S., K. (2023, May 16). LinkedIn. Linkedin.com. https://www.linkedin.com/pulse/understanding-law-vibration-how-your-thoughts-affect-life-selvakumar/

Samayla Jewellery. (2024, August 13). Manifesting with Crystals: A Guide to Attracting Your Desires. Samayla Jewellery. https://www.samayla.co.uk/blogs/samayla-blog/manifesting-with-crystals-a-guide-to-attracting-your-desires

Saxton-Thompson, C. (2020, April 22). *Evening Gratitude Practice - Wholehearted Life Therapy | North Palm Beach, FL.* Wholehearted Life Therapy | North Palm Beach, FL. https://wholeheartedlifefl.com/blog/evening-gratitude-practice/

Scott, A. (2015, March 11). The Power of - The 2X CEO - Medium. Medium: The 2X CEO. https://medium.com/the-2x-ceo/the-power-of-focused-intent-96d59ddfc4f5

Scott, E. (2020, November 18). Understanding and using the law of attraction in your life. Verywell Mind. https://www.verywellmind.com/understanding-and-using-the-law-of-attraction-3144808

Scripting for Manifestation: A Step-by-Step Guide - Centre of Excellence. (2024, February 8). Centreofexcellence.com. https://www.centreofexcellence.com/scripting-for-manifestation/

Scurio, J.-M. (2023, August 20). Thoughts, Emotions, and Intentions. Iloveureka! https://www.iloveureka.com/post/thoughts-emotions-and-intentions

Sesay, A. (2024, January 16). The Complete Guide to Oracle Cards. ELLE. https://www.elle.com/horoscopes/a46333458/best-oracle-card-decks-guide/

Sirivarangkun, W. (2020, August 16). 8 Best Meditation Apps of 2023 to Practise Calm and Focus. Mindful Wonderer.
https://mindfulwonderer.com/best-meditation-apps/

Sneha. (2023, February 21). Mastering the Art of Reality Shifting: How to Use Parallel Realities for Manifestation. Medium.
https://snehagm1207.medium.com/mastering-the-art-of-reality-shifting-how-to-use-parallel-realities-for-manifestation-%EF%B8%8F-f63fe478ef7f

Sood, P. S. (2021, July 6). *The 7 7-Day Meditative Manifestation Routine!* Linkedin.com. https://www.linkedin.com/pulse/7-day-meditative-manifestation-routine-parmeet-singh-sood/

Team Asana. (2021, November 29). 10 limiting beliefs and how to overcome them. Asana. https://asana.com/resources/limiting-beliefs

Tempera, J., & Talbert, S. (2022, March 27). *The 369 Manifestation Method Has Taken Over TikTok, And TBH, I Can See Why.* Women's Health.
https://www.womenshealthmag.com/life/a39518396/369-manifestation-method/

Tewari, A. (2022, June 12). *How to Effectively Write Affirmations and Practice Them + Examples.* Gratitude - the Life Blog. https://blog.gratefulness.me/how-to-write-affirmations-how-to-do-affirmations/

Thalia. (2023, July 3). 17 Guided Journal Prompts for Goal Setting | Notes by Thalia. Https://Notesbythalia.com/. https://notesbythalia.com/journal-prompts-for-goal-setting-and-reviewing-progress/

The 12 Best Crystals for Manifesting Your Dreams - Centre of Excellence. (2024, January 12). Centreofexcellence.com.
https://www.centreofexcellence.com/crystals-for-manifesting/

The Manifestation Collective. (2020, February 27). *How To Use Scripting To Manifest.* The Manifestation Collective.
https://themanifestationcollective.co/scripting-to-manifest/

The Science of Manifestation: How Visualization Can Help You Create Your Own Reality. (2023, August 30). WindowStill. https://www.windowstill.com/the-science-of-manifestation-how-visualization-can-help-you-create-your-own-reality/posts/

The Secret Witch. (2024, June 14). The Power of Mindset in Manifesting: Why Actionable Steps are Key to Achieving Your Dreams. Medium.
https://medium.com/@renatadaniel_60327/the-power-of-mindset-in-manifesting-why-actionable-steps-are-key-to-achieving-your-dreams-0bc3231e77ac

Travers, M. (2024, July 2). A Psychologist Explains The Phenomenon Of "Reality Shifting." *Forbes.*
https://www.forbes.com/sites/traversmark/2024/03/20/a-psychologist-explains-the-phenomenon-of-reality-shifting/

Travers, M. (2024, March 29). A psychologist explains the power of "vision boarding" for success. Forbes.
https://www.forbes.com/sites/traversmark/2024/03/29/a-psychologist-explains-the-power-of-vision-boarding-for-success/

True Vibes Unleashed. (2021, January 28). *True Vibes Unleashed.* True Vibes Unleashed. https://www.truevibesunleashed.com/pet-professional-blog/intention-setting

University of Miami. (n.d.). *Soothing Affirmations.*
https://fsap.miami.edu/_assets/pdf/Flyers/affirmations-and-breathing-exercise-handout.pdf

Urezzio, Jennifer. (2020, January 24). *Your Personal Formula for Manifesting Your Vision - Kind Over Matter.* Kind over Matter.
https://kindovermatter.com/your-personal-formula-for-manifesting-your-vision/

van Kempen, A. (2019a, January 5). The connection between Neuroplasticity and the Law of Attraction - Bujoo Academy. Bujoo Academy.
https://bujooeducation.com/academy/is-there-a-connection-between-the-law-of-attraction-and-neuroplasticity/

Velez, H. (2023, January 13). What Is Manifestation? The Good Trade.
https://www.thegoodtrade.com/features/what-is-manifestation-how-to/

Visualization meditation: 8 exercises to add to your practice. (2023, August 22). Calm Blog. https://www.calm.com/blog/visualization-meditation

Visualization to Calm Nervous System. (2023, September 23).
Www.cibdol.com. https://www.cibdol.com/blog/1643-visualization-to-calm-nervous-system

Walker, T. A., & FSU Contributor. (2020, April 9). *Mirror, Mirror on The Wall: Hey Future Self.* Her Campus.
https://www.hercampus.com/school/fsu/mirror-mirror-wall-hey-future-self/

Wander Art. (2023, August 2). 7 Steps to Personalized Positive Affirmations. *Wander + Art.* https://doi.org/1002956143/20230630_195254

Wellness design consultants. (2022, July). Wellness Design Consultants.
https://biofilico.com/news/2022/6/22/sound-therapy-for-mental-wellbeing-the-top-5-apps-to-know

Willgress, L. (2024, November 28). Best mindfulness apps in 2024 to keep calm during a crisis. The Independent. https://www.independent.co.uk/health-and-fitness/best-mindfulness-apps-a8217931.html

Williamson, I. (2024, October 20). Tesla's Code to the Universe: Understanding the 369 Manifestation Method. Linkedin.com.
https://www.linkedin.com/pulse/teslas-code-universe-understanding-369-manifestation-ipek-ev6rc/

Wooll, M. (2022, July 19). Don't let limiting beliefs hold you back. Learn to overcome yours. BetterUp. https://www.betterup.com/blog/what-are-limiting-beliefs

Zen, U. (2024). Insight Timer - #1 Free Meditation App for Sleep, Relax & More. Insighttimer.com. https://insighttimer.com/_ultimate_zen/guided-meditations/new-moon-meditation-solfeggio-frequencies-manifestation

Image Sources

1. Photo by Lucas Pezeta: https://www.pexels.com/photo/woman-spreading-both-her-arms-2529375/
2. Original author unknow; colored by Ivar van Wooning, CC BY-SA 3.0 <https://creativecommons.org/licenses/by-sa/3.0>, via Wikimedia Commons https://commons.wikimedia.org/wiki/File:Nikola_Tesla_Colored.png
3. Photo by Binti Malu: https://www.pexels.com/photo/photo-of-a-sign-and-eyeglasses-on-table-1485657/
4. Photo by Matthias Cooper: https://www.pexels.com/photo/woman-in-green-shirt-smiling-1062280/
5. Photo by Mikhail Nilov: https://www.pexels.com/photo/person-woman-art-creative-6932015/
6. Photo by Photo By: Kaboompics.com: https://www.pexels.com/photo/photo-of-assorted-crsytals-4040639/
7. Photo by Antoni Shkraba Studio: https://www.pexels.com/photo/top-view-of-a-woman-in-getting-tibetan-singing-bowls-treatment-6252137/
8. Photo by Andrea Piacquadio: https://www.pexels.com/photo/content-woman-in-empty-hall-looking-out-window-4376623/
9. Photo by Polina : https://www.pexels.com/photo/handwrting-letters-on-blue-sticky-notes-8709442/
10. Photo by Min An: https://www.pexels.com/photo/photo-of-man-looking-at-the-mirror-1134184/
11. Photo by Mikhail Nilov: https://www.pexels.com/photo/woman-in-red-dress-holding-fire-6931866/

12 Matthias Weinberger, Attribution-NonCommercial-NoDerivs 2.0 Generic CC BY-NC-ND 2.0 <https://creativecommons.org/licenses/by-nc-nd/2.0/deed.en> https://www.flickr.com/photos/51035610542@N01/58525360

13 Photo by Photo By: Kaboompics.com: https://www.pexels.com/photo/tranquil-woman-resting-on-yoga-mat-in-earphones-at-home-4498187/

14 Photo by Alina Vilchenko: https://www.pexels.com/photo/photo-of-person-holding-cup-3363111/

www.ingramcontent.com/pod-product-compliance
Lightning Source LLC
Chambersburg PA
CBHW072154200426
43209CB00052B/1222